Fashion Design:

Process, Innovation & Practice

Fashion Design:
Process, Innovation & Practice

Kathryn McKelvey
& Janine Munslow

Blackwell
Science

© 2003 by Blackwell Science Ltd,
a Blackwell Publishing Company
Editorial Offices:
Osney Mead, Oxford OX2 0EL, UK
 Tel: +44 (0)1865 206206
Blackwell Science, Inc., 350 Main Street,
Malden, MA 02148-5018, USA
 Tel: +1 781 388 8250
Iowa State Press, a Blackwell Publishing
Company, 2121 State Avenue, Ames, Iowa
50014-8300, USA
 Tel: +1 515 292 0140
Blackwell Science Asia Pty Ltd, 550 Swanston
Street, Carlton South, Victoria 3053, Australia
 Tel: +61 (0)3 9347 0300
Blackwell Wissenschafts Verlag,
Kurfürstendamm 57, 10707 Berlin, Germany
 Tel: +49 (0)30 32 79 060

First published 2003 by Blackwell Science Ltd

Library of Congress
Cataloging-in-Publication Data
McKelvey, Kathryn.
 Fashion design : process, innovation & practice /
Kathryn McKelvey & Janine Munslow.
  p. cm.
 Includes bibliographical, references and index.
 ISBN 0-632-05599-5 (softcover)
 1. Costume design. 2. Costume design –
Vocational guidance. 3. Fashion – Vocational
guidance. I. Munslow, Janine. II. Title.

 TT507. M384 2002
 d46.9'2–dc21

                                    2002033223

ISBN 0-632-05599-5

A catalogue record for this title is available
from the British Library

Set in Trebuchet by Marie Doherty, Havant
Printed and bound in Great Britain by
Ashford Colour Press, Gosport

For further information on
Blackwell Science, visit our website:
www.blackwell-science.com

Contents

Contents

Preface

As a book on fashion design, this has been very stimulating to create. It is interesting and difficult to try and place the right information on the page in a form that communicates clearly. There is so much that becomes second nature during a career in design and teaching. Putting yourself back in the novice designer's shoes requires some searching!

Fashion is fleeting. Decision making on the kind of examples included will always have pitfalls, potentially dating the book. But the examples are here to make points and the points will always be pertinent regardless of any changes in technology and upheavals in the industry.

Successful design is about **thinking** and communicating the thoughts, on paper, or wherever, and realising them through prototyping, solving any problems along the way. There will never be a substitute for **good ideas** and these must be the focus of problem solving.

All of the ingredients for successful design are contained herein, it is up to the individual to put their personal design stamp on the world, whether it be by becoming a known designer, by working for a retail chain, by supplying others with products, or by moving into new media and flying the 'fashion' flag; all areas are equally valid and require the same commitment and enthusiasm.

When starting out as a designer or student, try to dispel preconceived ideas about design, try not to start a project with the end product as the focus. Taking the journey prescribed in this book may well turn up surprises and delights that may never have been considered, leaving room for the new and innovative. If each element of the process is explored thoroughly the actual development should be very exciting and each solution always unique. The skill comes in allowing preparatory work to influence design; how much or how little is a matter for judgement.

The book is called *Fashion Design: Process, Innovation and Practice* and at the risk of being repetitive it works like this: the **process** has been demonstrated clearly enough and in enough ways for it to become well established. The **innovation** comes from thinking in different ways, having different approaches, by searching for something new and not settling for the 'tried and tested'. The innovation exercises may be used as often as desired. The **practice** is obviously the Fashion Careers and the Case Study; there is a lot of information here and the links between the careers and the common elements of design help to gain understanding and put the design well into context.

It is hoped that this book gives some indication of what is expected from the design process. Above all, it has been very broad in applying the process to investigating graphics and styling also.

As a student, one of the hardest aspects of study to come to terms with is the sheer volume of information to learn. Don't lose sight of what the short-term goals are. With every design project completed comes more experience. Career choices need to be made along the way as the paths that are possible are many. For instance, you could become a textile designer, or a fashion stylist, or a womenswear designer, or a fashion/graphic designer; whatever the choice it really is up to the individual and their skill and judgement.

Each aspect of designing fashion garments could be studied in its own right.

More than anything though, in design, there is no right or wrong solution to a design problem, it will always have a personal stamp upon it, as long as the solution fulfils the brief in a creative and relevant manner...

Enjoy the process, give time for innovation and you will love the practice!

Acknowledgements

I would firstly like to thank my family, Emily, Lucy and Jack, for their patience, and offer my thanks and love to Ian, who is always supportive and full of common sense. Thanks are also due to my mother and father for their continued enthusiasm and interest in whatever I have done, and Ian's mother and father for their help in giving me the time I needed by looking after the children.

Others I would like to thank are the staff in the School of Design at the University of Northumbria for offering help and advice when it was needed, and to Kevin and Fiona Hilton who have contributed some fine work to the book.

Students, both past and present, on the BA (Hons) Fashion Marketing course have allowed me to try out different approaches in design when teaching. In particular I would like to thank Elaine Anderson, Amanda Baker, Kathryn Cook, Nadine Counsell, Julie Davidson, Alice Davies, Melissa Davison, Mhairi Gibb, Lowri John, Claire Massheder, Stephanie Mitchell and Brett Roddis, and also the companies who trained them, for their contributions to the Fashion Careers section of the book. Thanks also to Carolyn Berry and Kate James for their work.

A final thank you is due to my publisher, Richard Miles and his team, especially Caroline Savage, for the opportunity to produce this book, which has been an enjoyable and stimulating learning experience.

This book is dedicated with love to my father, Alexander McKelvey, 1926-2001.

Kathryn McKelvey

I would like to thank Neil and my sons Benjamin and Laurie for their support and patience, and all the staff and students of the Fashion Marketing BA (Hons) Degree course at the University of Northumbria, Newcastle.

Finally, I would like to dedicate this book to the memory of my late father, Stanley Hunt.

Janine Munslow

Introduction

The very word fashion signifies change. This pace of change shows no sign of halting and designers are under constant pressure to maintain their creative momentum. New developments in mass production and information technology have helped to increase this speed of change by decreasing the lead time between design and finished stock entering the retail environment, quickly turning catwalk fashion into high street equivalents. Brands spread their influence, constantly diversifying into new product areas. In such an arena there is a need for well-trained designers and other personnel to take up a variety of related career paths such as buyers and stylists.

Universities and colleges run degree courses and other specialist courses to provide a solid grounding in fashion education. This book is intended for anyone aspiring to a career in fashion and design.

There are so many approaches to designing clothes and so many factors to take into consideration that many beginners are daunted by the prospect; this book sets out basic principles and exercises in order to make fashion design a logical process, providing limits from which to expand skills steadily. This design process can be learned.

It should also be emphasised that there is more than one path to take when developing designs and it is the individual's input and the forming of their personal philosophy which helps to decide on the path taken. This philosophy develops with experience as does the ability to tell good design from bad, how materials are best used and handled and what is a long-term trend or a fad. Lack of experience need not be a barrier; being observant and aware of what is happening in the world can feed into design. Being enthusiastic, keen to learn and having an enquiring mind is a necessity.

The book presents an overview of what is involved in studying and becoming a designer in the contemporary fashion industry. It is intended to show the breadth of the industry rather than in-depth views of any particular area. For reasons of size it does not set out to be, nor could it be, fully comprehensive in its contents. Its aim is to pull together in one textbook the basic knowledge and skills necessary to begin designing. Once some experience has been gained in design, the book sets out the possible career paths that graduates of design can enter.

The various stages of the design process from colour to embellishment are investigated. Colour is an enormous part of what makes a design work and can be dealt with only in very simplistic terms here because the book is published primarily in black and white.

In addition research inspiration, direction, design development, how to plan collections and ranges and promotion are also covered.

This book uses a variety of problem-solving approaches to encourage the development of innovation, experimentation and versatility. What is often referred to as 'flair' is analysed through a logical approach so that anyone can improve their skills with the exercises included. The innovation section can be applied to virtually any area of design and product development and the exercises can be used over and over again.

The design process indicated here of research, development and prototyping is as valid for the promotional and graphical side of design as well. The ideal would be that this process becomes second nature to the designer.

The analytical problem-solving approach is illustrated in a case study located in the second half of the book, where a hypothetical design brief is developed from concept to product and promotion, setting

Introduction

out the skills and strategies utilised. More emphasis is put upon paper-based development, with the beginnings of prototype development. It is inevitable that the case study will date, and some other examples also, due to the nature of the research material, the fashion direction and final designs, and the silhouettes, print and pattern. However, the basic process still holds true. We have endeavoured to use classic and simplistic designs as examples that illustrate a point rather than complex designs.

Consideration is also given to the portfolio and a chapter deals with the types of career available within the fashion industry in an attempt to provide some sort of direction to graduating students, or students who are taking up work placements within the industry. The careers are written as if the graduate is just beginning their career so that titles such as assistant designer or assistant buyer are used.

Because we are dealing with the basic design process there is not space here to discuss pattern cutting in depth. However, pattern cutting is an implicit part of the process and, as with many other areas discussed, it could be that 'creative cutting' and construction is the direction that one may take as opposed to designing garments that are, for example, 'print based'. Often the amount of construction included in garments becomes a 'fashion' issue as does the input of all the other areas mentioned. Further reading into pattern cutting is recommended.

There are many books on the theory of design. Questions concerning what makes a good design or what is good taste are part of an ongoing debate in the design world. This book tries to avoid semantics where possible in order to simplify the process, to be practical, but does try to place fashion in a contemporary design context.

Opposite is a simplistic flow chart indicating the way the book works in explaining the design process and also the logical progression of the process from researching ideas to choosing a career in the industry.

Introduction – Flow Chart

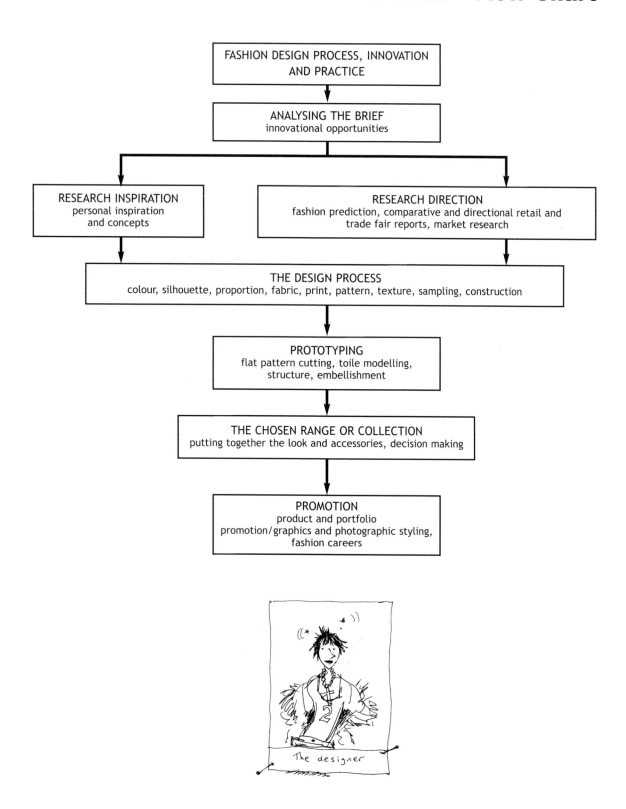

FASHION DESIGN PROCESS, INNOVATION AND PRACTICE

↓

ANALYSING THE BRIEF
innovational opportunities

RESEARCH INSPIRATION
personal inspiration
and concepts

RESEARCH DIRECTION
fashion prediction, comparative and directional retail and
trade fair reports, market research

THE DESIGN PROCESS
colour, silhouette, proportion, fabric, print, pattern, texture, sampling, construction

↓

PROTOTYPING
flat pattern cutting, toile modelling,
structure, embellishment

↓

THE CHOSEN RANGE OR COLLECTION
putting together the look and accessories, decision making

↓

PROMOTION
product and portfolio
promotion/graphics and photographic styling,
fashion careers

The designer

Analysing the Brief

Before work is begun, it is very important to understand exactly what is required for a client or project. Reading a brief and carefully dissecting it can make the difference between a success or a failure. Asking the right questions is essential!

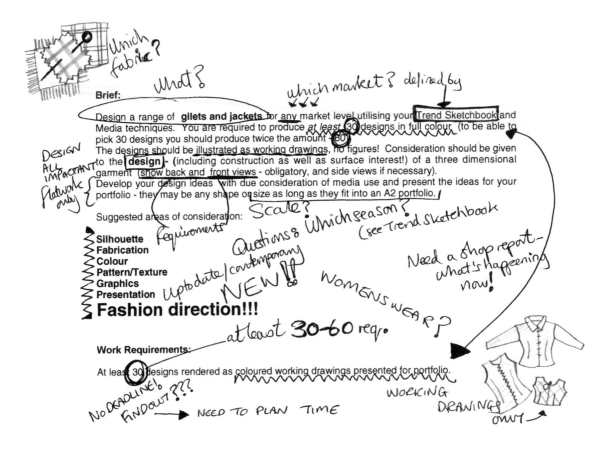

Brief:

Design a range of **gilets and jackets** for any market level utilising your Trend Sketchbook and Media techniques. You are required to produce at least 30 designs in full colour (to be able to pick 30 designs you should produce twice the amount - 60).

The designs should be illustrated as working drawings, no figures! Consideration should be given to the **design** - (including construction as well as surface interest!) of a three dimensional garment (show back and front views - obligatory, and side views if necessary).

Develop your design ideas with due consideration of media use and present the ideas for your portfolio - they may be any shape or size as long as they fit into an A2 portfolio.

Suggested areas of consideration:

- Silhouette
- Fabrication
- Colour
- Pattern/Texture
- Graphics
- Presentation
- **Fashion direction!!!**

Work Requirements:

At least 30 designs rendered as coloured working drawings presented for portfolio.

Handwritten annotations: Which fabric? What? Which market? delivered by — Brief. Design all important. Flatwork only. Scale? Requirements. Questions: Which season? (see Trend Sketchbook). Uptodate/contemporary NEW!! WOMENS WEAR? Need a shop report - what's happening now! at least 30-60 req. No deadline! Find out??? NEED TO PLAN TIME. WORKING DRAWINGS only.

What are you being asked to do?

How are you expected to do it, in terms of format, presentation, and layout?

How much work is expected?

Have you been given a deadline?

Can you impose a timetable of tasks?

How will you break down the tasks?

Is a shop report necessary to gain a better understanding of the market?

Is the shop report going to be directional or comparative?

Do you need to look at other material such as: historical, cultural, artistic inspiration?

Which season are you designing for?

Are there any special considerations, for example designing children's nightwear?

What will you use for fashion direction?

Are there any magazines that you need to refer to?

What type of fabric and finish are required?

Do you have to source the fabric as well as choose it?

Do you need to include samples of finishes?

Have you got a firm idea about the colour story, fabric story, silhouette, details, pattern and texture?

What style of execution is required?

Are you free to interpret the chosen market in the way you see fit?

Can you use inventive presentation and media techniques?

Analysing the Brief

By Dr Kevin Hilton

The analysis of a brief should start with deconstruction but end with reconstruction. Breaking down a brief allows you to try to determine what the client believes they want and, more importantly, to identify what the client actually needs. Briefs can often be ambiguous when the client attempts to describe what they may feel the issues are.

If you look at riddles and lateral thinking questions closely, you will notice that there are often three types of content within a question/brief structure:

- **Key elements**, which frame important points positively or negatively.
- **Situational elements**, which are of secondary importance but help to set the context for the key elements.
- **Distracting elements**, which serve only to distract from the key elements.

Distracting elements must be identified quickly and discarded in order to clarify the structure of the brief and to identify the key elements. Once these are determined, the brief needs to be reconstructed with a clear context, described by situational elements, setting the scene for designers and the client to then understand the key elements. Sometimes it may help to use association and metaphor if situational elements rely too heavily upon specialist experience for the key elements to be fully understood.

Once you have written a clear context for the brief and taken a design or innovation approach to the process, you will need to conclude the brief by qualifying your intent with an 'Actions List', for the benefit of the designer as well as the client.

It should be noted that there are two different approaches to this deconstructive and reconstructive process of brief analysis. Design takes a problem identification approach which is a reactive approach, looking to identify and solve key problems to create a better product or service. Innovation, however, takes a proactive approach by opportunity identification, to change the way user needs are served by products or services, avoiding problems through the innovation.

In order to deconstruct and reconstruct a brief, with either a design or innovation approach, it may become apparent, especially within an innovation context, that more market knowledge is required in order to proceed with any certainty.

From your first pass at reconstructing the brief it should become apparent what research direction is required. Try drawing up a mindmap to clearly log your approach and research findings. Start the map with the key opportunities and/or problems and then begin to expand upon these with related issues. As your research continues in parallel and your comprehension of the market-area opportunities improves, you will need to transfer the new information to the map to keep it up to date. There are many different approaches to mindmapping, the divergent approach being most common, but try a networking approach by creating links between those issues that are related to more than one element. By this networking method you may become aware that some of the apparently minor issues are quite key to a lot of elements within the whole context.

The mindmap acts as a reflection point, but you will need other tools as part of your process; for instance try creating a generic checklist of issues that will need attention. Also, always keep a notebook close at hand for data, questions and ideas. Short-term memory is often unreliable.

Your research approach should be fully logged with images, swatches, reference material and other relevant data, neatly filed for quick reference and clearly written so that anyone reading the project can easily determine your present position and how you got there.

Innovation

By Dr Kevin Hilton

This chapter describes the process of innovation in a series of steps that are intended to help you appreciate what innovators do, and to show you how easy it is to become an innovator. Here is a definition:

Innovation is when an inventor develops a product or process, which successfully changes the way we do things.

There are two types of innovation. There is *original* and *incremental*. An example of original innovation would be the Sony Walkman because there was nothing quite like the Walkman prior to its production and it has changed the way people listen to music in public. An example of incremental innovation would be a Vauxhall Zafira because whilst it is an additional people-carrier in the marketplace, it has changed the way space can be used inside a vehicle by the way that its rear seats can be folded down flat for storage.

Innovation runs in cycles where the successful original innovation may get incrementally innovated many times before its marketplace eventually disappears because either the need ceases, or because we develop another original innovation that totally changes the way we do what we did before.

The process of innovation may also have a number of cycles within it. For instance, the process of dreaming up a possible solution may take place a number of times before you are happy to proceed to the next step. You may also run a number of prototypes of a concept before you are satisfied you have a design that someone would want to buy.

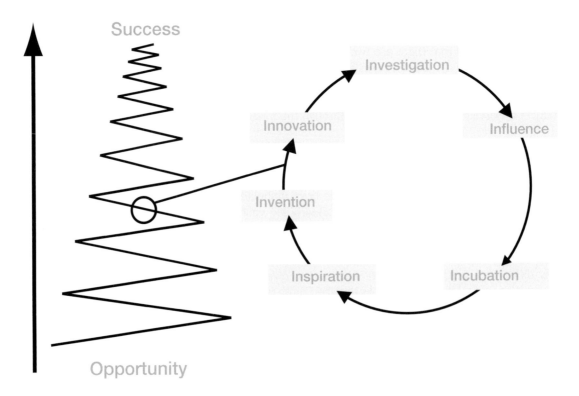

The innovation cycle describing the innovation process

Innovation

OPPORTUNITY

Innovators and problem solvers try not to look at problems with a negative frame of mind; instead they try to view them as opportunities to help people, to prove their ability to innovate and possibly to gain some reward. If you can identify an opportunity, which is experienced as a problem by a number of people, and if you feel it is something you could create a solution to, you may decide to take up the challenge.

An innovation is something that is developed and introduced to the problem area and which changes the way that things are done. You wouldn't call your idea of how the problem could be solved an innovation, you wouldn't even call your idea a solution until you have tried it out and proved that it worked. However, you would be able to call your idea a potential innovation if you knew that the solution could mean that people might do things differently and, most importantly, that they would be happy to do so.

There are different methods for identifying opportunities. You may choose to be 'reactive' and wait until you have a problem, or until you see someone else having a problem, or read about people having a problem. You may chose to be 'proactive' which means actively searching for problems, by searching through newspapers, or by generating lists of problems from themes. For example:

Opportunity identification list

GENERATION THEME: Icy weather
PROBLEM OPPORTUNITIES: People slip
           Locks stick
           Pipes freeze
           Ears ache
           Birds starve
           ...

INVESTIGATION

If a problem is not simple, requiring an obvious solution, then it is complex requiring an original solution. Complex problems require sufficient knowledge and skill before they become realistic opportunities.

When we try to solve a problem we use a number of methods to identify a potential solution. We may use our experience: Have we ever dealt with a similar problem before and how did we do it? We may use the experience of other people: Do we know someone who may help us to solve the problem or do we know of a book or video that would give guidance? We also find ourselves using what is called 'tacit knowledge' which is when we know certain facts but we don't remember where from. We may also find that we don't actually know for sure that something is correct, just that it feels right. This is called intuition.

To get on top of the problem you must investigate it properly before you proceed towards a solution, or you could find yourself wasting time with blind alleys. So think smart from the beginning and remember this phrase for problem solving:

'Investing time at the top avoids a pain in the bottom.'

Innovation

In order that you stand the best chance of success with solving a problem or developing an innovation, you need to be aware that there are many things that may influence you and some will be covered now. It is important that you keep a positive frame of mind, because innovations often do not become a success without perseverance which in turn needs self-motivation.

The important thing to remember about influences is that we are all individuals and what may influence one person, positively or negatively, may not influence another person in the same way. So you will benefit from seeing what works best for you.

Some people cannot think creatively if they are distracted; they need to find somewhere to work where they can concentrate, away from the phone and television for instance. Some people are the opposite and thrive off activity and distraction because when their minds are distracted good ideas come to them from their subconscious.

Well-being is very important to clear thinking. If we are exhausted, or unwell, the time is not right to be thinking about solving a problem, even if you are committed to providing a solution. Forcing yourself to concentrate is counterproductive to quality solutions. Stress is an important issue to consider also. The difference with stress as an influence is that not all stress is bad for all people. Whilst stress will stop some people from thinking straight, it will motivate other people to get on and solve the problem.

Motivation is best when it is self-generated rather than when coming from other people. If you find you are losing interest in a problem you might want to stop altogether, but if you have already committed a lot of time and energy to the project, that would be a waste. So try thinking about the challenge in a different way, tackling it by a different method, maybe getting other people involved. Keep it fun.

Experience comes through maturity and the taking of opportunities to develop knowledge and skills. You cannot be expected to know everything, ever. You should look upon the role of the innovator as being a 'manager of opportunity'. If you do not want to be a specialist innovator, dealing with specific types of opportunity, it is better to learn broadly and to turn to others when you need specific knowledge and skills.

Diet may influence us; even when we feel fit, certain types of food can improve our mental and physical abilities. For instance the reaction time of our nervous system can be improved by eating fresh fruit and vegetables. The oils in fish can help with thinking and memory because they contribute to the maintenance of nerves involved in information storage and retrieval. However, certain foods have potentially negative effects. For instance whilst sugary foods can give us a short-term energy high, this is usually followed by a low which is more likely to make you critical than creative. There are two important rules to bear in mind concerning a diet:

'Correct diet is not about eating less. It is about eating responsibly.'
'Seek qualified advice before you enter into a new diet plan.'

Sense of humour has benefits for most of us, and not just for problem-solving situations. Humour helps us to remain positive, by laughing off mistakes, and helps us to cope with stress. It also helps us to communicate and to bond with other people socially. It can help to suspend criticism of the ideas being generated and it allows us to think about the weird and abstract ideas. By generating associations and scenarios, which may not always be the solution we are looking for, we may provide 'stepping stone' ideas which help us to reach the solution we are after.

INFLUENCE

This is the stage in the innovation cycle when those involved put the most energy into gaining an even greater understanding of the problems involved. This stage is about discussing all related issues, generating ideas and testing them out.

Communication is very important throughout the innovation process. You need to be able to clearly communicate your intent. If you cannot explain your idea clearly it will be misunderstood, which will result in your idea being compromised or dismissed.

So, drawings with annotation make a good start, whether you are presenting your idea or just making notes. Also make sure that you date all your notes and keep them filed neatly for reference. You may also wish to use a 'confidentiality agreement' with those you involve with your potential innovation. (Never hand over original notes to people, no matter how helpful they promise to be. Keep originals, send copies.)

Generating ideas could take the form of dreaming up concepts whenever you get a spare moment, but it is much more fruitful if you generate ideas during an organised session. Concept generation sessions, or 'brainstorms', involve between two and eight people, plus one person whose role is facilitator. It is the facilitator's role to get the session rolling by showing a funny video clip and/or asking a lateral thinking question, or something similar, for the first 5 or 10 minutes. Then with the intention of getting as many ideas as possible from the group the facilitator delivers the main question. As people begin to generate ideas, the facilitator makes sure that the 'no criticism' rule is obeyed and that the group does not wander too far off subject. (It is permitted to wander a little, as this can allow the group to return to the problem from a different angle.) The facilitator must also keep motivation up when ideas start to flag and this is best done by having a list of approaches to the problem, for example:

Concept generation session approach list

PROBLEM:	Lock stuck with ice
APPROACHES:	Things the lock could be designed to do to stay ice free
	Things you could put on the lock to melt the ice
	Things you could do to prevent the lock icing up
	Locks that don't require keyholes

The session should be run in a room with no phone distractions or interruptions. However, the room should have plenty of natural light and, if possible, an interesting view out of the windows because it is good to provide sources of visual stimulation, which may also include images and models on show inside the room. Refreshments, e.g. drinks and confectionery, should be available throughout, not just for breaks but also as an energy source. The session length may vary, dependent upon subject matter, but a session should not be shorter than 1 hour because it takes 20-30 minutes for people to settle down to the flow.

Whilst it is good to generate workable solutions during such a session, if people only say things they believe are workable then their mental blocking of certain ideas may preclude others from being sparked off on a workable solution path. In addition to the production of a mass of potential solutions, brainstorming also serves to charge up the subconscious to continue thinking about the subject as a background process.

INCUBATION

This is a strange stage in the process, in that all the other stages require that those involved in the innovation process actively concentrate on the problem issues. However, for the success of idea incubation we need to divert our conscious mind from the subject of the challenge. This may be achieved in one or more ways. You could just work on something entirely different, or go for a walk, take a bath, go out for the evening, read, watch television or sleep. Some of these ways work better for some people than for others.

Innovation

Whatever you decide to try, the intention is to give your subconscious a chance to add ideas to those that the conscious mind has generated during the brainstorm. This may not happen overnight. It could take days, weeks, even years, as the subconscious waits for the needed piece of information to fall into place so that it can make the desired association. There are no guarantees of inspiration from incubation within a set project time-frame. Incubation is a stage that may help, but is difficult to avoid; even if you try going straight from brainstorming ideas to testing them, the subconscious will still be attempting to incubate the information it has available.

INSPIRATION

Inspiration cannot be guaranteed, which means you cannot guarantee that you will provide an innovative solution. You might find a solution to a problem without inspiration, but you cannot create an innovation without the stage of inspiration, no matter what impact/sensation is experienced as the light dawns. For a solution which will significantly change the way people do things, the inspired solution is unlikely to be an obvious association, no matter how simple it may appear on reflection.

INVENTION

Unfortunately, the completion of this and all previous stages is still no guarantee of success. The inspired ideas need to be developed into prototypes for evaluation. It is only when a working concept is developed that you can claim you have an invention.

Once you have an invention, you may wish to obtain Intellectual Property Rights for it, which will put you in a more favourable position when looking to gain agreements for manufacture. However, there is much to consider before applying for rights. For example, patents take many years to be granted, if granted, and if your innovation is time sensitive it might prove better to forego the rights path and get it into production as soon as possible.

INNOVATION

Only when an invention is developed into a design and is specified for manufacture can the invention reach the mass market. Then only when it has experienced success in the marketplace for an extended period and users have successfully adapted to its new way of doing things, can it be qualified as an innovation. Whilst this stage then becomes success, in the innovation cycle it also returns to investigation, as market feedback on the innovation allows for incremental improvements and the cycle starts again.

SUCCESS

Success of an innovation can be measured in a number of ways: the income it generates, the number of people it helps, the level of impact on society, its life-span, the number of other innovations it sparks off and the pride it brings the inventor. The image of success is important to the potential innovator right from the start of the challenge, for without it they lack the fundamental motivation we call 'vision'.

PERSONAL INNOVATIVE POTENTIAL CHECKLIST

The following checklist is intended to improve your awareness of factors of influence upon personal innovative potential. Our potential to be successfully innovative fluctuates from day to day and also depends on the time of day. The checklist covers background experience, external factors and internal factors and helps determine whether it is a good time to be involved in creative activities when the checklist has been run, and also helps determine things that need improving to increase chances of success at that moment.

Checklist for personal innovative potential

Please read through the whole questionnaire, then take a few moments to consider the potential influences upon your personal innovative potential (PIP) before starting to answer.

For your present situation, from 1 for negative up to 7 for positive, how would you rate the following:

The value of your background experiences:
1. Puzzles and constructional toys? (Brainteasers, jigsaws, Lego, etc.)
2. Interests? (Scientific, technological, creative, etc.)
3. Practical knowledge? (Woodwork, metalwork, etc.)
4. General knowledge? (Historical, topical, etc.)
5. Occupational variety? (Full-time, part-time, etc.)

Your immediate state of:
6. Mind? (Clarity, confidence, communication, etc.)
7. Health? (Fitness, energy, appetite, etc.)
8. Spirits? (Motivation, humour, emotions, etc.)
9. Surroundings? (Safe, stimulating, comfortable, etc.)
10. Companionship? (Supportive, dynamic, imaginative, etc.)

To calculate the PIP: 1 to 3 = 0, 4 = 2.5, 5 = 5, 6 = 7.5 and 7 = 10

Signed: Dated: Score:

It should be noted that an individual's results from different days may be compared but no meaningful comparison may be made *between* individuals because the rating of the different factors is very subjective. Besides, the adversaries are not the colleagues, they are the challenges.

Successful innovation is about creating the future by identifying opportunities and then, through the abilities of 'thinking outside of the box' and managing the knowledge and skills required, to inspire the associations needed to succeed in the marketplace.

The following broad factors influence the potential of an individual to successfully innovate as part of an incremental process of problem solving during the stages from opportunity identification to the success of the product or service.

(1) Broad and broadening, background experience.
(2) Motivation towards concept generation and problem solving.
(3) Teamworking, being more effective than group working.
(4) Appropriate use of humour for social levelling and inspiration.

Exercises to Promote Innovation

By Dr Kevin Hilton

BRAINSTORMING

As mentioned earlier, under the heading 'Influence', brainstorming, or concept generation, can be a valuable 'first action' exercise.

REVIEW AND REFLECTION

Throughout a project, you should have designated points for reflection upon work to date, whether this is a review of ideas generated by a brainstorm or a review on completion of a project stage. Such reviews require the use of constructive criticism, and are intended to check and discuss the project for opportunities to improve further upon what has been achieved, or even the way it was carried out. This approach is known as total quality management and can be a valuable management tool.

To carry out a review of a brainstorm or project stage you will need a copy of the brief, your theme or action list and a list of criteria which states exactly what the project needs to address in order to fulfil the brief. With these, you will gain a measure of worth for ideas generated or how well the project is keeping on track.

ENQUIRY EXERCISE AND MOTIVATION

For any activity or process to become second nature it requires regular practice. However, in order that you practise regularly you need to be motivated to do so and this can only come from within. You must determine what sort of mental, physical and spiritual experiences you have an interest in whilst keeping an open mind to try new things.

A major influence upon personal innovative potential is background experience. Unfortunately, such experience is absorbed over time and cannot be gained so easily at short notice. What follows is a series of exercise types intended to suggest sources of stimulation that can improve your approach to opportunity identification and problem solving.

ALTERNATIVE USES

This exercise can be used as a short warm-up before a brainstorm. Take an item from home or the office and see how many alternative uses you and your colleagues can think of for it within 5 minutes. This exercise can be done either as a group or as a competition between two halves of the group. This exercise can also be done individually but it is best not to run it as a competition between individuals because it is easier to cope with being part of a losing team than it is being an individual loser.

ASSOCIATIONS AND SCENARIOS

Working alone or in a small group, take pairs of ideas and place them in association. Consider whether these associations could describe novel concept services or products. If not, try again with other ideas until workable concepts are generated. Then develop scenarios (story lines) around the use of each concept. This exercise is similar to brainstorming, but instead of the intent being to generate large numbers of ideas, this exercise is intended to help develop an approach towards the evaluation of ideas, which improves the individual's ability to identify opportunities.

TWENTY QUESTIONS

This exercise is sometimes called 'Animal, Vegetable or Mineral'. With a limit of just twenty questions that can only receive 'Yes' or 'No' answers, the first three questions are best spent determining what mix of materials the puzzle item is made of. This game may have been played as a child with the goal of guessing the item with the least number of questions asked.

Exercises to Promote Innovation

However, there is an additional part suggested for this version: the person posing the puzzle should think about the questions and the method of questioning that their opponent is using and consider how the questioning could have been more effective. The person trying to solve the question should consider how best to narrow their field of focus quickly and also consider whether there are any additional clues their opponent has unwittingly given away. For example, does the opponent keep looking towards the same part of the room or is there a trend to the puzzle items they keep setting?

LATERAL THINKING PUZZLES

There are a number of puzzle books available as source material for this exercise and whilst they are usually structured so that you can puzzle over them alone it is much more fun to do this exercise in pairs or groups. This exercise has some similarity to 'Twenty Questions', though it is not usual to impose a limit to the number of questions asked during such puzzles. However, you may wish to impose a limit. It is also suggested that you should be thinking about the effectiveness of questioning as the puzzler or the solver. Thinking of what to ask when you first begin such exercises is often more difficult than you might expect, but as you practise you begin to develop an approach and the exercise becomes more fun.

HOW THINGS WORK

Although you may think of this exercise in terms of product, it also refers to services. This is an exercise in enquiry, which may include how a sewing machine stitches or how a franchise works. Such a line of enquiry improves our understanding of the world around us when we answer our enquiries, and when we are unable to answer a question our mind stores the enquiry, sometimes for years, and improves our attention to these issues. Improvements in alertness may develop a sharpened perception of opportunities.

WHY THINGS DON'T WORK

Similar to the above exercise but approaching from the opposite direction this requires that you consider why products or services fail. There are often opportunities to be had from failures, even your own. 'Do not fear failure. Respect it.' Many lessons cannot be learned without failure. (You have no idea how well a car can hold the road in wet or icy conditions until you feel it begin to skid.)

NATURAL PHENOMENA

Though you can find books that pose such puzzles as these, you can spot examples of such phenomena yourself, and it is very important that you do so. Use this exercise like the previous two to sharpen your perception and to motivate an attitude of enquiry. Some explanations may simply be gained from an expert source, whilst other explanations will be developed as this exercise sparks off a research exercise. See 'Diary or Log-Book' on page 14.

A DAY IN THE LIFE OF ...

This is a social exercise where you are encouraged to increase your knowledge of other professions by taking the opportunity, socially, to enquire about a typical day for people you meet. Many people will make a mental note of people's professions by title only, but you can increase the depth of your experience and confidence if you carry out a regular exercise of 'A day in the life of ...'.

HAVE A GO

This is also an exercise in experience building, but it differs from the previous in that you are encouraged to try things for yourself, provided they are not physically dangerous. Try cooking a meal for ten, redesigning your garden, or reading a classic novel. You may seek supervision for this exercise. You might think about recording your experiences; some experiences may be suitable for video.

Exercises to Promote Innovation

DOING THINGS DIFFERENTLY

Try doing something you have done many times before in a different way. Question in what way was that better or worse than normal. Create new experiences and compare these to old ones on a regular basis.

MAGIC TRICKS

For this exercise you should start with a magic trick you have seen and try to recreate it from scratch. Ask yourself: Was it achieved by device or distraction? Can you do it alone? How would you best go about such trickery? This is a very practical type of exercise but nonetheless requires some thought.

ANALOGIES

The more you practise the use of analogy the more it will help with many of the other exercises, whilst improving memory recall and perception of opportunities. Analogies sometimes allow you to make inspired leaps through 'If-Then' reasoning. If you suggest something is comparable to your puzzle problem, then following the analogy further there may be additional similarities, which may suggest possible solutions to the problem at hand. Analogies are also a good means of explaining new concepts to people.

KNOWLEDGE TRANSFER

The best way to learn about something and to better understand it is to teach it. By verbalising your thoughts, you will often find you can think more clearly about the subject. This is not just because you may not wish to pass on incorrect information, but because individual thinking and learning styles handle visual, auditory and kinaesthetic information differently, and the more types of referencing your brain can make the easier it will be to recall this information on demand. So, for this exercise, when the opportunity arises pass on some of your knowledge. You may get some in return.

DIARY OR LOG-BOOK

Keeping a diary or log-book with you at all times will encourage you to note down ideas, information and questions. You cannot be expected to remember all thoughts that pass through your short-term memory, but you will find that writing them down helps transfer them to long-term memory as well as providing a back-up in the log. This is more an exercise in recording information than one of thinking.

SUMMARY

You need to be motivated towards practising any of these exercises, and some may appeal more than others, so start with those first. You don't have to try them all to feel the benefit. It may help not to think in terms of exercises, which sounds very academic. Think of them as a source of fun. So, if they aren't much fun then they probably aren't the right experiences for you, yet.

There are plenty of opportunities open for everyone to improve their knowledge and processes for innovative thinking, within education and professional practice, using the techniques described here. However, to do well, individuals must be intrinsically motivated. Intrinsic motivation comes from within, driven by personal purposes.

Developing Designs – Quickstart Exercise

BEGINNING TO DEVELOP DESIGNS

The key to good design development is good research material that actually means something to you, that is, you have chosen it because you see a way in which it may be developed or utilised. As the process continues, different skills are required and personal judgement, decision making, is needed to select ideas that need to be developed.

From the following flow chart choose one or more elements from each level to **begin** designing. Remember, if you have analysed the brief and already have some parameters to work within, your choices should be easier to make. Removing any preconceptions about the end product allows for a more innovative and stimulating process and allows you to be more versatile and open-minded in your designing.

LEVEL 1

PERSONAL INSPIRATION & CONCEPTS

Look at:

- Films
- Exhibitions
- Galleries
- Museums
- Books
- Magazines
- Architecture
- Photography
- Theatre
- Travel
- The Internet

RESEARCH DIRECTION

Look at:

- *Textile View*
- *View on Colour*
- *Interior View*
- Worth Global Style Network
- *International Textiles*
- *The Collezioni Series*
- Prediction companies, if you have access
- The Internet

RESEARCH

Look at:

- Trade fairs
- Trade exhibitions
- Directional retail report
- Comparative retail report if you have a product to begin with!
- Mintel and Keynote statistics
- Graphics
- Promotional styling

LEVEL 2

DESIGN DEVELOPMENT ON PAPER

Look at:

- Shape/silhouette
- Volume
- Proportion
- Scale
- Exagerration
- Cut/construction
- Colour combinations

TEXTILES

Look at:

- Colour
- Print
- Pattern
- Surface decoration
- Texture
- Weaves
- Hand painting
- Combinations of two or more of the above

TECHNICAL DEVELOPMENT IN 3 DIMENSIONS

Look at:

- Colour combinations
- Samples of finishes
- Samples of details
- Fabric finishes
- Pattern cutting
- Working on the stand with fabric-draping, pleating, sculpting

Research Inspiration

IDEAS AND INSPIRATION

Starting to collect research material will provide a focus for your thoughts and provide material from which to start generating ideas. Collect colour schemes, articles, sketches, fabrics, notes, scraps of wrapping paper, wallpaper, advertisements, photographs, trimmings, articles, sewn samples, memorabilia, postcards, old patterns, etc. Collect stills, video, animation clips, music and graphics to make a digital scrap-book. Remember that one idea leads to another ...

Research Inspiration

Where do ideas come from? Ideas can come from anywhere, they can be completely original and connected to the designer in a very individualistic way, or they can be influenced by the current *Zeitgeist* (spirit of the time) as part of ongoing trends.

Sources of inspiration may be related to the designer's personal experience; they can come from museums to ink blots, from the Internet to family photographs. Listed below are some of the more well-known sources of inspiration.

Books and magazines: The most obvious reference point for information and photographic style. It is important to remember that magazines have a three-month lead time on publishing. Newspapers are a good source of up-to-the-minute design trends, catwalk news and fashion comment. Trade magazines provide information on new developments in fabric technology, etc.

Art: New art movements are influential in that they question the boundaries of what we perceive to be acceptable. Artists comment on our contemporary values. Art can be inspiring in its capacity to be shocking, beautiful, witty, new, conceptual or challenging.

Graphics and photography: These can provide a rich source of inspiration both for design and illustration purposes.

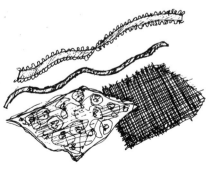

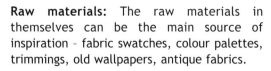

Raw materials: The raw materials in themselves can be the main source of inspiration – fabric swatches, colour palettes, trimmings, old wallpapers, antique fabrics.

Research Inspiration

Exhibitions: Any exhibition can be inspiring; however, there are certain large exhibitions that are influential in that they capture the common imagination. During the last 30 years there have been exhibitions of Native American, Mexican, Egyptian and French art that have had a direct influence on fashion design.

Travel: Alternative cultures are traditional areas of inspiration. Specific cities or countries become inspirational because of social change, avant-garde artistic movements or 'happening' street culture.

Cinema: Cinema has a huge impact on design, often capturing the spirit of an age succinctly; think of *Bonnie and Clyde* in the 1970s, *Mad Max* in the 1980s, *Titanic* in the 1990s to name a few examples.

Architecture, furniture, interior design: These have long-term impact on contemporary design ideas. Design philosophies like 'minimalism' start here.

INTELLIGENCE GATHERING

As explained previously, inspiration for design can be derived from many non-related areas. Design needs to be informed and consider current and forward-thinking developments in fashion. Garments need to be developed, produced and bought ahead of the season for retailing, so it is essential that any content is right for that season.

There are a variety of sources that can aid this intelligence-gathering process.

Street style: Using an individual or group sense of style as inspiration. (See 'Sub-culture/Street Style' later in this chapter.) Sketching or photographing stylish clothing worn by passers-by is an interesting exercise as fashion is as much about how looks are put together as individual designs, particularly as there is a current vogue for individualism and customised styles.

Trends: As these are affected by the continuing action of economic, social, political and cultural changes, they can provide essential design direction for the designer.

Fashion prediction material is part of this and is invaluable in finding a direction in an area unfamiliar to the designer. Often the designer will have their own instinctive idea about direction but support from such fashion prediction consultancies can be helpful.

Designers: Analysing catwalk collections, looking at the seasonal developments of designers who are currently the most influential. What makes them directional? Designers from the past who are going through a retrospective. Other areas of design can be useful, for example menswear.

Retail: Most designers research garments through designer shops and stores in order to see and feel at first hand other designers' work. This can involve travel to the fashion capitals of the world.

New media: Technological advances in new media have created a rich graphic resource and the ability to access a global exchange of visual information (the Internet!) has revolutionised the designer's field of vision.

Research Direction – Fashion Prediction

Fashion prediction material can provide much of the direction required to inform the design process. Such material is available as limited edition publications from consultancies and as general fashion periodicals available in magazine format.

Originally, fashion prediction material emerged to try and homogenise fashion markets, so that designers and manufacturers could provide fashionable merchandise that would appeal broadly in the marketplace.

This has led to a blanding of the high street, where designers' labels are copied and reproduced cheaply at various levels of the market and the original is no longer so distinguishable.

The consumer now wants more from their clothing and has fragmented into a variety of guises - they are multi-faceted and have no desire to look and behave exactly like their contemporaries. This creates problems for designers, as they have to get to know the new consumer.

However, this does not mean that fashion prediction information is redundant; on the contrary, it is as important as ever in giving direction regarding the consumer, lifestyles, customer profiles, catwalk shows, street style, retail reports and, last but not least, trends. The designer has the responsibility of interpreting trends for their customer. The designer may find this information in prediction periodicals and publications.

Prediction consultancy publications and prediction periodicals – what are the fundamental differences?

PREDICTION CONSULTANCY PUBLICATIONS

Promostyl, Trend Union, Carlin, Here & There are examples of prediction consultancies who traditionally produce limited edition books that are regularly sent to clients every month or so. They generally sell annual subscriptions to clients (designers, retailers, manufacturers) which will include a number of customer consultations. Clients are invited to presentations of designer collections and directions for a new season. The subscription tends to be very expensive due to this personal attention. The books contain a lot of hand work; approximately 500 would be produced and could cost, for example, £5000 for 12 monthly publications including a variety of presentations and consultations.

PREDICTION PERIODICALS

Examples of prediction periodicals are *Textile View, International Textiles* and *Trend Collezioni*.

Periodicals tend to be less expensive, for example around £95 per year for four quarterly issues of *Textile View*. They are more general in format and are ideal as inspiration for a variety of personnel. They give an overview of a season and include edited highlights of designer collections. They provide general information regarding markets.

COLOUR FORECASTING/DESIGNS

Research Direction – Fashion Prediction

Fashion prediction consultancies are a relatively recent development, many appearing in the 1960s – many claim to be the first. They tend to be quite small, occasionally employing extra designers and illustrators when the trend prediction/forecasting issues are due for publication.

Syndicates develop new colour palettes and themes seasonally and sell this information to the prediction companies. Some prediction companies develop their own themes by analysing previous seasons' developments.

Consultancies and periodicals cover the following fashion markets:

Menswear, womenswear, childrenswear, knitwear, accessories, printed textiles, casualwear, sportswear, jeanswear and any other areas as they become relevant.

Periodicals such as *Viewpoint* are dedicated to the changing consumer and general trends and work in tandem with sister publications such as *Textile View*.

TREND PREDICTION

Trend prediction information is much broader than 'fashion prediction' in that it may not be specifically related to fashion. Trends are recorded and trend predictors (looking for patterns of human behaviour, indicating changing markets or new consumer needs) constantly monitor the media and society.

Many industries use trend prediction to forecast relevant changes and plan product development, for example the interest in all things spiritual was forecast by Faith Popcorn, initially in the 'Popcorn Report' and was developed and continued in 'Clicking'.

Spirituality is seen in the interest of such things as 'Feng Shui' which is a popular approach to interior design. Bookstores now have shelves dedicated to spirituality, as individuals look inward to discover themselves in a fast-moving world.

The fashion prediction consultancy relies on experts in a variety of fields for its structure. They have personnel all over the world to help in gathering intelligence.

The full-time staffing of a consultancy generally consists of the **editor** who creates

CATWALK COLLECTIONS

the company philosophy. The **publisher**, on the technical side, puts the information together. The **retailing** and **merchandising** professionals and **fashion directors** work on consultancy for individual clients, by applying the general fashion trends more specifically to their needs. They must be skilled in, and aware of, a variety of markets. This could, for example, involve developing exclusive collection strategies, concepts and designs for spinners, weavers, textile printers, men's, women's and children's garments, shoe and accessory manufacturers and for retailer's private labels. They may also be expected to sell subscriptions to the publications to new clients.

Research Direction – Fashion Prediction

The prediction consultant can be working on a number of seasons at any one time!

The objective is to work closely with the client to determine their concerns, goals and potential customers with a view to tailor-making a design solution.

The success of prediction companies relies on pinpointing trends and developing these for individual markets at the *right* time! Trends may be affected by social, cultural, political and economic moods, as well as evolutions in lifestyle, technological developments, media and retailing. This information is tapped and recorded by **international correspondents** who provide up-to-date intelligence from fashion capitals, such as London, Paris, Milan, New York, Florence and Tokyo.

The design team determines how this intelligence affects fashion and consumer awareness.

Designers/Illustrators are employed with design skills in menswear, womenswear and childrenswear, and illustration skills in interpreting and developing silhouette themes, knit and woven samples, print stories and accessories. They *visualise* new ideas developed from the trend information and consider carefully figure proportions and stylisation so that any personnel, using the service, can understand what is suggested by the visuals.

International agents promote and sell the service to clients worldwide, for example in Los Angeles, Tokyo, London and Paris.

THE PREDICTION YEAR

The prediction consultant's year is quite involved and complicated because of dealing with information from a variety of seasons. For example they predict about 18 months to 2 years ahead of time. But they also include information from fabric fairs which is needed to design and produce collections that are shown 6 months before they are shipped to retailers, so that orders can be taken and the product can be manufactured in plenty of time.

Follow-up collections blur the boundaries of the traditional seasonal breakdown of a year. Samples of merchandise, actually in the stores, are used to show some clients the design of a particular item that may be directional at their market level.

COLOUR

Colour is the first consideration of a season and is produced for autumn/winter and spring/summer ranges.

The colour is put into dye 18 months ahead of the specified season (some clients may require this information up to 2 years earlier, but this may not be shown in the final presentation box).

Fibre and fabric manufacturers require advanced information regarding colour as they have to develop their product early enough for designers and garment manufacturers to buy it and in turn develop their product. Presentation packs are usually presented with a fixed range of colour and a removable range so that clients can develop their own colour combinations. Colour packages are included in the subscription price and may be sold separately to clients who only require colour information and not the rest of the service.

Then follows the setting of the **mood** for a new season by developing **fabric** and **silhouette** themes.

SILHOUETTE & FABRIC

Research Direction – Fashion Prediction

Prediction consultancies produce a variety of materials and publications for their clients.

Directional themes and full-figure silhouette illustrations of menswear, womenswear and childrenswear together with accessories are shown. Included in the publication may be exclusive handlooms for wovens, knits and prints produced by freelance and in-house designers.

COMMERCIAL FABRICS may be published at this time, derived from fabric fairs such as, Premiere Vision, Interstoff and Prato. These are created from hand cut and stuck swatches of directional fabrics relating to the season's previously predicted themes.

POSSIBLE DESIGNER COLLECTIONS REVIEWED
- Milano Collezioni Uomo, Milan.
- French couture collections, Paris.
- French menswear designer collections, Paris.
- American menswear collections, New York.
- Men's and women's designer collections at Spanish Fashion Week, Madrid.
- Milano Collezioni Donna, Milan.
- British designer womenswear collections at London Fashion Week, London.
- French womenswear designer collections, Paris.
- American womenswear designer collections, New York.
- A variety of markets at Graduate Fashion Week, London.

The 'reportage' would be in the form of photographs.

Occasionally certain fashion 'centres' are more popular than others. This would be reflected in the quality of 'intelligence gathering' by freelance staff.

COVERAGE OF FASHION FAIRS
Fabric fairs: Premiere Vision, Paris; Interstoff, Frankfurt; Comocrea, Cernobbia, Italy.
A variety of shows will be visited such as: 40 degrees, London; Filofuture, Idea Maglia, Moda In & Tessuto Accessori, Milan; Prêt-à-Porter, Salon de la Lingerie, Interfillière, Paris.

RETAIL REPORTS are conducted all over the world with a view to finding 'directional' garments in

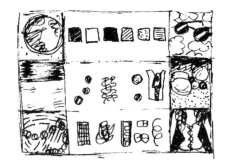

MOOD & INSPIRATION

the retail sector. Flat drawings of these can reassure clients about what is happening elsewhere and may be adapted for their market. The information includes: resource, designer, price, fabrication, colour and any unique selling points as well as detailed sketches of the garment.

SAMPLE DIRECTIONAL GARMENTS are bought from all over the world and sent to the main studio. The garments are analysed and illustrated as specification drawings in the publication. The prediction company retains the sample garments so that clients may view fabrication, proportion, detail, colour or manufacture.

Research Direction – Fashion Prediction

Prediction companies also offer added extras giving value for money.

Added extras include:

- A **retail directory**, including new and existing retail outlet information, is often provided of major cities.
- **Technical drawings** of the designer collections.
- **Basic designs** derived from the main predicted themes.
- **Slide packages** of the key directions derived from the designer collections.
- **Photographic coverage** of street fashion.

Included in the subscription price may be a range of services such as:

- Access to up-to-date **fabric libraries** with fabrics and trimmings from Europe and America.
- A limited number of **consultations** regarding the development of a client's range or collection.
- **Audio/visual presentations** at the start of a new season.
- Other **specialist publications** offered may be: Sweatshirt/T-Shirt, Casual Sportswear, Jeanswear, Layette, Baby, Child, Junior, Active Sportswear, Skiwear, Beachwear, Footwear, Accessories, Hosiery.

SILHOUETTE

THE FASHION PREDICTION DESIGN PROCESS

One publication is worked on at a time (there may be 12 – one a month, or more, depending upon the size of the consultancy and its breadth of expertise).

A company that develops its own thematic material will hold a succession of meetings with the core team resulting in decisions being made regarding the amount and content of the themes for a particular season, including evocative names. This is achieved by discussion. Each individual states what they feel will be a strong trend in the coming season. Where one idea is repeated by several members it is incorporated into the plan for the book. Where similar ideas are mentioned they are amalgamated to form a strong and identifiable trend.

A colour palette is decided upon. The colours are divided into groups corresponding with the themes. Some colours unavoidably overlap, but as main and accent colours alter the overall impression, each theme is sufficiently different.

Research Direction – Fashion Prediction

The designers then start designing. The walls are covered with tear sheets from magazines, separated into appropriate themes as inspiration. Photographs from the trade fairs are used for guidance on design details.

Fabrics are then discussed in conjunction with the designers designing the garments. It is important to consider the balance of outerwear and separates fabrics. When decided, lengths of fabric and any interesting accessories are ordered to provide swatches for the books.

After the designs are completed they are illustrated with reference to particular markets and 'lifestyles' and to capture the 'essence of the themes'. Technical drawings are also produced, either by the design team or by freelance illustrators.

Samples of knitwear and new textiles may be commissioned which will be photographed for the books.

Mood boards, containing visuals, fabric and trims, depicting the themes, are completed. The mood boards are sent away to be photographed and return as transparencies.

During the process of compilation, agents worldwide will have been securing old and new clients, to whom the books will be sent on completion. A master copy of the book is compiled and sent to the printers to have a sample copy printed and bound. The copy is checked for any mistakes before the book goes into production.

Travel is an important aspect of fashion research and visiting trade fairs allows reports to be compiled which observe not only trends apparent from the exhibitors' displays, but also from the people (who are mainly from the fashion industry) as they walk around the shows. This exercise helps to understand the differences in international fashion, which is important when catering for foreign clients.

THEME DEVELOPMENT

Fashion prediction for a new season is usually promoted as a series of 'themes'. These are designed to inspire and direct the designer for a number of markets. Themes, often, are given names to evoke feelings and moods and reflect the content of the theme. Each theme may appeal to one or more markets and requires interpretation from the designer to develop for their particular market. Often the prediction company offers some consultation to the designer which is helpful in this development.

Markets are usually defined by the cost of the merchandise. Nowadays the markets referred to have vague names such as boutique, fashion aware, better end, pm dressing. This is more reflective of changes in 'lifestyle'.

These can be interpreted into customers buying from:

Lower market – budget; lower middle – high street, chain stores; middle – independent labels and department stores; upper middle – designer diffusion; upper – designer.

Research Direction – Fashion Prediction

TAILORED STRIPES

SUMMER HOLIDAY

Fashion prediction themes have often been very literal in their nature: **nautical** would show striped sweaters and sailor hats; **utility** would always involve dungarees of some description and multiple pockets. A **chic, tailored look** may well involve a French beret.

It is important that visual codes are identifiable and mean similar things to different people.

UTILITY

The illustration must work hard to convey a mood, an attitude, in the pose, that convinces the viewer about the sort of person that is being targeted.

Similarly, a **total look** is always helpful because accessories can contribute to not only the communication of the theme, but may also convey the type of person who would wear the 'look'.

It is important that the proportion is believable and that the information is clear.

Research Direction – Fashion Prediction

Themes nowadays are less literal and are more about mixing ideas together to create something fresher. 'Lifestyle' has become important, consequently themes may be put into an evocative setting which helps to create the correct mood. Less clothing detail is on view but the message allows the designer to make their own interpretations.

TECHNO NERDO

ACTION ORIENT

COOL CARMAN

DESERT

VEGAS

VEGAS ADVENTURE

Drawings derived from illustrations by Gary Kaye in *Textile View 42*

New uses of technology have resulted in the development of the **Worth Global Style Network (WGSN)** who produce a comprehensive on-line service to the fashion industry. Members pay an annual subscription to view the full site; students may visit an educational version free of charge (for a limited period). The services available are: news updates daily; women's, men's, youth and children's trends; city reports from London, Paris, Milan, New York and Tokyo plus seasonal reports from new and trend-setting areas; international trade fair calendar; lifestyle reports – consumer attitudes, evolving buying patterns, seasonal phasing; catwalk shows and trade event reports; graphics libraries; resource listings; licensing reports – brands, films, sports events; mailbox problems and solutions; technical and production news – garment and fabric technology, dyeing and finishing, print techniques, footwear and leathergoods technology.

Research Direction – The Fashion Cycle

Fashion design does not exist in a vacuum, it must be considered in the context of other contemporary design diciplines and issues. Whether its speed of change is inspired or fuelled by the 'trickle down' effect, that of designers and brand domination of the marketplace, or the 'trickle up' effect, that of street fashion and consumer power influencing catwalk designers. Fashion is inextricably linked to the general trends in design, reflecting the social and cultural milieu of the times.

The divisions in the fashion industry between the made-to-measure, luxurious fabrics and exacting techniques of haute couture and the range of levels from 'Designer' ready-to-wear collections, exclusive, niche and volume mass market level, are easy to identify. Where the boundaries are less clear are in the divisions between art and fashion and at the opposite end of the scale between individual style and fashion.

Fashion cycles have been likened to waves, in that as one wave is dissipating another is forming; there are many cycles happening simultaneously, for example the silhouette may change more slowly than the colour or length. Fashions, fads and trends all go through a beginning, middle and end phase, considered to be avant-garde when ahead of its time through levels of popularity until after a certain period of time the look becomes dated and old-fashioned. These fashions languish forgotten until they are discovered, become interesting again to the early adopters of fashionable trends and enter the cycle once more, as either inspiration for a new fashion, re-invented as a retro look or worn as pure vintage style.

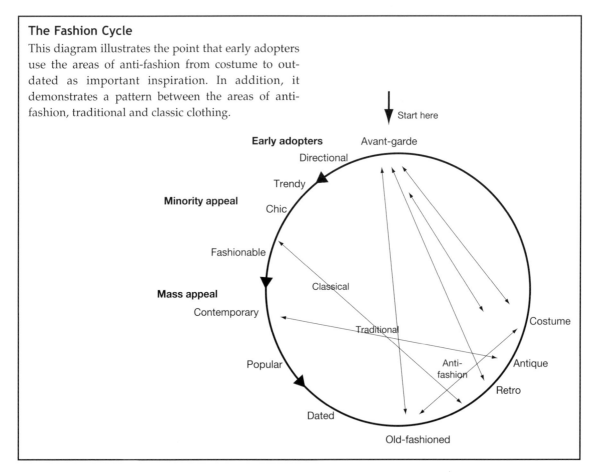

The Fashion Cycle
This diagram illustrates the point that early adopters use the areas of anti-fashion from costume to out-dated as important inspiration. In addition, it demonstrates a pattern between the areas of anti-fashion, traditional and classic clothing.

Research Direction – Fashion and Art

When does fashion become art, when does art become fashion? Throughout the 20th century an exploration of the parallels between these two worlds contributed to the development of visual culture and to the way in which fashion was perceived and created. It is important to understand this process in order to appreciate the complexities of contemporary fashion design and its symbiotic relationship with art.

The design of clothes had traditionally been regarded as a craft rather than an art form but its status has risen over time. The relationship between fashion and art developed through the 20th century with an explosion of artists using clothing as a metaphor for the human form or spirit. This history of cross-pollination culminated in 1996 at the international 'Florence Biennale', where artists and designers collaborated to explore the relationship between art and fashion. This influential exhibition provided the forum for debate and inspiration for a new generation of artists and designers who have shaped the way in which fashion design has developed and now contributes to our visual culture.

The associations between art, clothing and cloth have a long history; this section can only be a brief overview of key moments in Western art and design. There are many wider influences; for example, during the 1880s Native American Indians painted their muslin garments with images of vision-inspired art. These sacred motifs were believed to be capable of variously giving protection from bullets or bringing back the buffalo.

Although the great couturiers Worth and Poiret had worked with artists at the end of the 19th century, it was the Arts and Craft movement that paved the way for the radical change in dress that would be a practical alternative to the cumbersome costumes of luxury *haute couture*. The right conditions were created for the emergence of modern dress and the opportunity for modern art to play a role in this revolution. An early exponent was the painter and inventor Mariano Fortuny who experimented with an alternative style of dress, an early form of minimalism where the relationship between the cloth and the body was explored. His signature pleats were influenced by Greek sculpture.

During the early 20th century, painting changed totally when cloth became more than a surface for holding paint. Braque and Picasso began to use it in their paste-ups and collages, followed by other artists like Duchamp, Man Ray and Kurt Schwitters. In the 1920s Sonia Delaunay introduced the radical ideas of the Constructivists to fashion, emphasising the importance of abstract pattern taken from cubist paintings and applying this to patchwork techniques, thus making the individual garment an art form.

Initial explorations by Dadaists melded with fashion in the influence of surrealism on designers such as Elsa Schiaparelli who became friends with Jean Cocteau and Salvador Dali, from whom she commissioned designs for fabrics and accessories. She experimented with innovative materials – cellophane, glass, plastic – and created witty, sophisticated statements with her padlocked suit belts, exposed zippers and musical purses. Her signature colour 'Shocking Pink' was taken from the artist Christian Bérard.

The couturier Charles James working from the 1930s to the 1950s was a master of construction and crossed the boundary into sculpture using mathematical principles, engineering skills and experimental use of new fabrics like rayon. He looked upon his designs as works of art, which were made from precisely constructed interchangeable components.

During the 1960s and 1970s designers responded to the new emphasis on youth culture in parallel with the experimental and challenging developments in the art world. Paco Rabanne experimented with new materials (paper, plastics and metal) and his first collection was entitled 'Twelve Unwearable Dresses'.

Research Direction – Fashion and Art

In the 1980s new movements such as 'Wearable Art' and 'Conceptual Clothing' began to take shape alongside the use of clothing in performance and installation art contexts. The Wearable Art Movement concerned themselves with clothing the body and the spirit, while the making of the cloth concentrated on embellishment and fabrication.

In the early 1980s the Japanese designers Kansai Yamamoto, Yohji Yamamoto and Rei Kawakubo caused a storm in the Western fashion world by challenging our accepted view of the relationship between clothing and the body. These designers came from a tradition where there was no clear-cut distinction between art and craft. Kawakubo anticipated lifestyle design and marketing by creating her garments as part of a total environment, designing her shops as meticulous installations rather than the expected retail environment.

Further explorations were made by de-constructionists during the mid-1990s. The design work of Martin Margiela and Anne Demeulmeester had a revolutionary effect upon the development of fashion design. Martin Margiela examined the stages of construction in a process used by the Russian formalists known as 'laying bare the device'. The process of construction through toiles and construction stages and techniques was laid bare in the finished garment.

As traditional forms of painting and sculpture had given way to conceptual work and other genres, these further explored the use of clothes. Couturiers also reinvented themselves, as artists in there own right. Issey Miyake is an example of a designer whose work is elevated beyond the constraints of seasonal trends through his consideration of the balance of influences of East and West, and the continued exploration of the relationship between the linear, geometric shapes created from his innovative textiles and the human form.

An area of special interest to artists has been traditional needlecraft, collage and quilt making. Artists have used this ancient method of extending the life of cloth by sewing together remnants to create a metaphor for the human body or spirit. A notable example is Maggie S. Potter's 1978 'Label Jacket' created solely from old garment labels in the manner of a friendship quilt. Tracy Emin takes an extreme strand of contemporary art that uses intimate details from the artist's own life as a subject matter. By using her self-image to advertise brands like Vivienne Westwood and Blue Sapphire Gin, she straddles the worlds of art, fashion, marketing and media, which further influence our visual culture.

Transformation, the idea that garments can morph into a series of alternative forms, was initially explored by designers like Issey Miyake but has continued to be a subject of interest. The artist Lucy Orta's exploration of the relationship between objects such as tents and coats and other elements of survival wear has affiliations with fashion designer Hussein Chalayan's influential show which featured garments that transformed into chair seat covers and tables.

The interaction of contemporary fashion and art is now so synonymous that it is hard to imagine that it has not always been so. The use of art in advertising and the bricolage of artistic references in our clothing have created a visually sophisticated consumer whose purchasing power also interacts in the process of design.

'Modern art's new sights are part of glamour, part of fashion and they fit with the spirit of now.'
Mathew Collings (2000) *This is Modern Art*,
Seven Dials, Cassell and Co., London.

Research Direction – Sub-culture/Street Style

Sub-cultures and street style have always provided a fertile ground for experimental and unusual clothing. Style is central to sub-cultural identity; clothing and adornment are a way of broadcasting belonging, loyalty and alternative viewpoints.

Groups such as Beatniks, Skinheads, Rockers, grunge, rave and cyberpunk have all provided a rich hunting-ground of ideas for designers, but more importantly they have influenced mainstream fashion by the 'trickle up' factor. These alternative styles have influenced the way we dress through: constant appropriation, as elements of individual style are popularised by exposure to media; the relaxing of formal dress codes; and the emphasis on individual style that has encouraged a pluralistic style of dress.

Before we can begin to analyse the design process it is important to view fashion in a contemporary context and in terms of its relationship to marketing and the media. Many fashion garments in magazines today owe less to the designer than to the stylist or photographer. Contemporary fashion is as much about style and two-dimensional image as it is about cut, fabrication and construction.

Sub-cultural references have been borrowed liberally as consumers become more sophisticated and knowing in the interpretation of these styles and messages. Street style is often the term used to describe the creative way people wear this mix of clothing, purchased either on the high street, or from retro or recycled sources. A new generation of magazines has become established over the last 20 years that celebrate the style statement of the individual. Today's consumers have the freedom to interpret ready-made clothes how they like. This non-classifiable but highly individualistic style of dressing has become the opposite of the uniformity of the postwar era.

An early example of this 'trickle up' process was Yves Saint Laurent's collection for Dior in 1962, inspired by the Rocker and alternative Beatnik styles of the Paris Left Bank that were emerging at that time.

Fashion designers now use a mix of extracted elements from sub-cultures, street style, historical reference, cross-cultural, utilitarian and fantastical elements in a true post-modern style, catering for the current vogue of eclecticism. Often the very styles that developed as an alternative to high fashion become highly fashionable themselves.

Designers continue to exploit both the energy and creativity of the street and the iconography of sub-culture in order to layer meaning through irony or authenticity into their collections, whilst conversely influencing mainstream and alternative fashion cycles.

Design Process – Introduction

This chapter of the book attempts to explain the process involved in making design decisions. It is a complex process to unravel and one that is personal to the designer in question. The design process, which results in a three-dimensional outcome, needs to consider all the following areas:

- Colour
- Silhouette
- Proportion
- Construction
- Fabrication
- Prototypes
- Embellishment

Each of these areas is discussed as separate sections within this chapter. These basic elements provide an initial framework from which to expand into more complex design considerations.

For the professional designer commercial and market considerations must be taken into account. The manufacturer wants something that can be produced economically. The retailer wants volume sales and eye-catching styles. The consumer has demands on many levels from clothes worn as a complex series of non-verbal communications to social status, sex appeal and the more practical considerations of fit, value and ease of care. The designer has to please everyone.

When considering a design brief, the market level and price points are essential in deciding the way in which your design development will progress. It must look good – is it aesthetically pleasing? Is it an appropriate use of materials? Is it fit for the end purpose? Although the designer has to consider all these issues, for the aspiring designer it is essential to experiment with the basic principles and to develop an appreciation of how all these individual elements work together to provide good design solutions.

Every stage of the design process involves some sort of graphic notation and the sequence usually follows the same route: design brief, investigation, ideas for solutions, chosen solutions, realisation and evaluation.

Design Process – Introduction

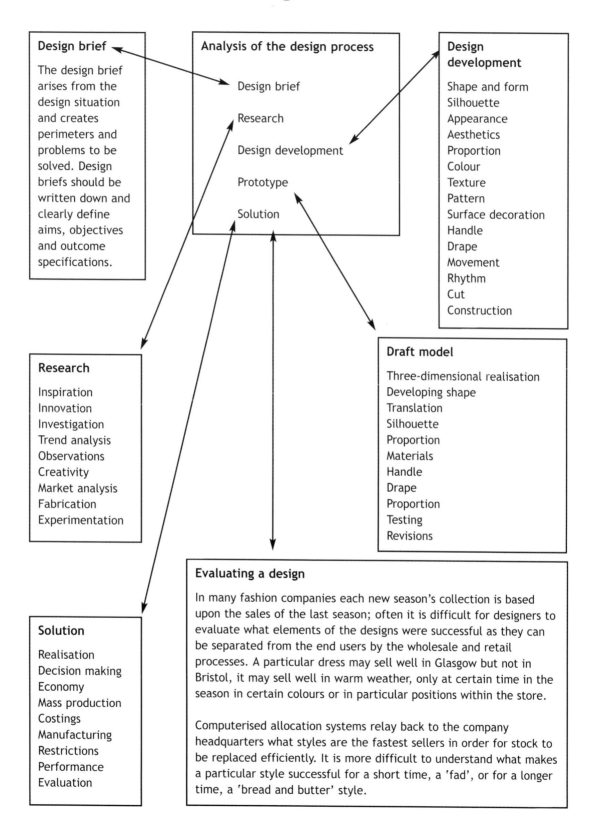

Design brief

The design brief arises from the design situation and creates perimeters and problems to be solved. Design briefs should be written down and clearly define aims, objectives and outcome specifications.

Analysis of the design process

Design brief

Research

Design development

Prototype

Solution

Design development

Shape and form
Silhouette
Appearance
Aesthetics
Proportion
Colour
Texture
Pattern
Surface decoration
Handle
Drape
Movement
Rhythm
Cut
Construction

Research

Inspiration
Innovation
Investigation
Trend analysis
Observations
Creativity
Market analysis
Fabrication
Experimentation

Draft model

Three-dimensional realisation
Developing shape
Translation
Silhouette
Proportion
Materials
Handle
Drape
Proportion
Testing
Revisions

Solution

Realisation
Decision making
Economy
Mass production
Costings
Manufacturing
Restrictions
Performance
Evaluation

Evaluating a design

In many fashion companies each new season's collection is based upon the sales of the last season; often it is difficult for designers to evaluate what elements of the designs were successful as they can be separated from the end users by the wholesale and retail processes. A particular dress may sell well in Glasgow but not in Bristol, it may sell well in warm weather, only at certain time in the season in certain colours or in particular positions within the store.

Computerised allocation systems relay back to the company headquarters what styles are the fastest sellers in order for stock to be replaced efficiently. It is more difficult to understand what makes a particular style successful for a short time, a 'fad', or for a longer time, a 'bread and butter' style.

Design Process – Design Development

In order to make use of the basic principles outlined in this chapter it is important to know how to develop your thoughts on paper in order to fully expand an initial concept. The process of drawing your ideas not only records the thought process but, by constant experimentation, generates new ideas.

After collecting together your research, swatches of fabric and samples, a suitable figure can be sketched. The pose and attitude of the model will have an impact on the designs that you draw. If the figure is too stylised there is the possibility of getting the proportion wrong. If the figure is too life-like the design may lose its edge, its sense of individual style.

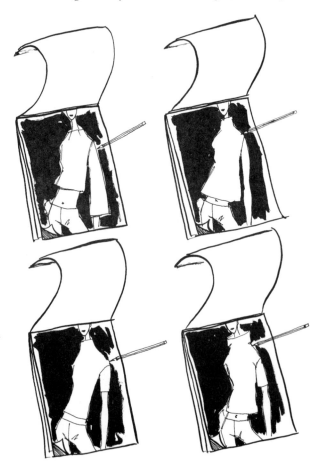

This is one popular way of working:

Using a layout pad or simliar translucent paper, trace your design ideas over the figure, varying the structure and silhouette. This allows you to concentrate on developing design ideas rather than on drawing the figure correctly every time.

In order to choose your best ideas you need to be judgmental but optimistic, be clear about direction but original enough to take on new ideas. It is easy to go the tried and tested route. Good ideas may take some time to hatch or it may take time to get into a different mind set. For example when a new look presents itself it is often challenging and initially looks 'wrong' aesthetically in some way.

Design Process – Design Development

When you are happy with the results complete the same process using form and shape to play with proportion, style or fitting lines in order to create a working structure.

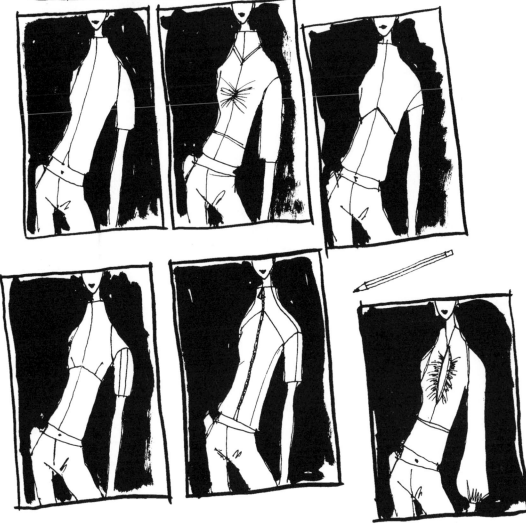

Design Process – Design Development

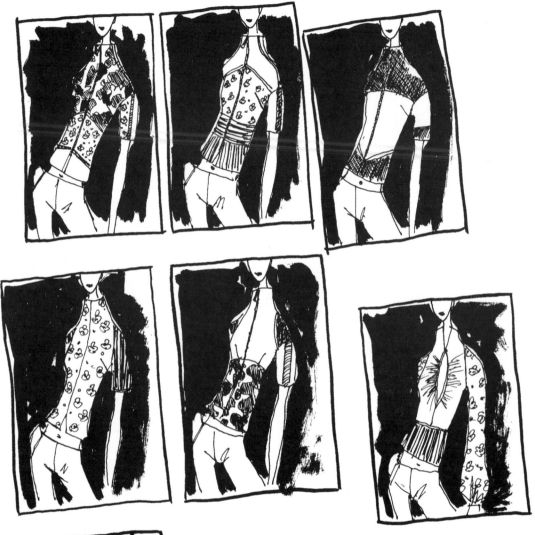

Finally, when you have considered the best results of your experimentation add the surface decoration, detail and finish.

At all stages consider the selected fabrics, trim, and colour palette.

Design Process – Design Development

The fabrication and colour can be considered at any stage but it is worth remembering that this element has often more impact than any seaming or detail. The finish is often overlooked as it is more difficult to draw accurately.

Samples should have been tried out using the fabrics and these can be pinned to the sheets in order to illustrate the kind of finish that is intended.

Design Process – Design Development

To bring your ideas to fruition you need to be enthusiastic and responsive. You need to be positive, persistent and ready to respond positively to any shortcomings.

It is common for even very creative people not to make the best of this phase. They are often uncertain, self-critical and see weaknesses as a lack of talent, instead of a need for more work or a different approach.

The next section describes the design process and use of colour.

Design Process – Colour

Colour is a fundamental consideration in the design process. It is often the first element that is noticed about a design and influences how that garment or collection is perceived. Colour is often the starting point of the design process.

Prediction and forecasting companies research and develop colour stories from many sources including international fabric fairs where yarn technologists, leather suppliers, trimming merchants and other related industries have developed new colour stories from existing colour palettes. The textile industry continually develops fabric technology in order to create fabric with innovative weaves, knits, texture, handle, drape and finishes. It is important to consider colour along with texture, as the surface of the fabric is integral to our experience of the colour itself.

Inspirational trade magazines discuss new colour trends in relation to key influences of the moment and give specific colour guidelines for use in textiles, fashion, cosmetics, interiors, products and graphics. They include interviews with people from different design disciplines, and articles giving background information on changing lifestyle, design and creative thinking. Specific colour palettes are suggested and are referenced from a commercial colour system, for example 'Pantone'. Pantone is an internationally recognised colour referencing system where thousands of shades are numbered and contained in a pack. This is vital in an industry where digital communication screens and printers are not accurate enough in representing original colour.

Often at the research and design development stage it is not about the description of a shade or hue but about patina. For example there are many variances of white – clear, pure, limed, chalk, whitewash. At the other end of the scale there is the intense saturation of shocking pink and fluorescence. Named colours can be useful in describing shades and surface, for example 'Oil black', 'Blackboard', 'Cloud black', 'Liquorice'.

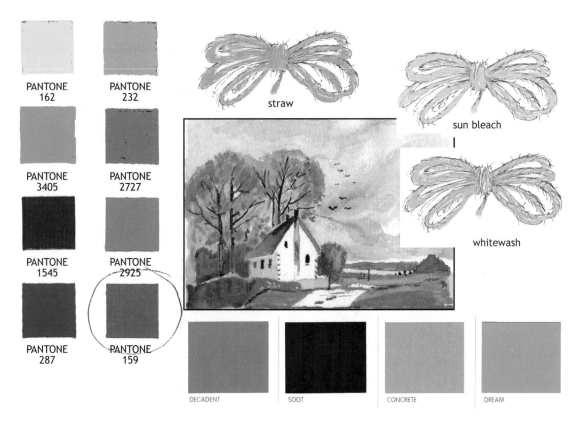

PANTONE 162
PANTONE 232
straw
sun bleach
PANTONE 3405
PANTONE 2727
PANTONE 1545
PANTONE 2925
whitewash
PANTONE 287
PANTONE 159

DECADENT
SOOT
CONCRETE
DREAM

Design Process – Colour

Colour is the property of an object that results from the reflection, transmission or emission of light waves which cause a visual perception in the eye depending upon the specific wavelength involved. In the case of paints, inks, and dyes, which contain pigments, their colour is determined by the light which is reflected. Each colour has a different wavelength or frequency. These are not in themselves coloured; the perception of colour comes from the eye or brain.

Colours are perceived differently when placed next to each other; generally brighter colours can seem larger than darker ones.

Colour can be said to have the strongest visual impact of an object; for example, warm colours and pure colours appear nearer, cool colours appear to recede. Light colours expand; dark colours contract. Yellow is perceived as the largest colour, black the smallest.

Colour can be described in terms of hue, value and intensity:

- Hue – describes a colour's position on the colour wheel.
- Value – describes lightness and darkness.
- Intensity – describes brightness saturation or impact.

Age diminishes the ability to distinguish the properties of colour.

THE COLOUR WHEEL

There are twelve segments of the colour wheel starting with red at the top. The primary hues of red, yellow and blue form an equilateral triangle within the wheel.

The three secondary hues of orange, violet and green stand between, forming another triangle, followed by red orange, orange yellow, green yellow, blue green, violet blue and red violet, which form the six tertiary hues.

A number of other terms are used to describe colours:

- Tint – a pure colour mixed with white; for example red + white = pink.

- Shade – a pure colour mixed with black; for example; blue + black = navy blue.

- Patina – the surface texture of the described colour.

- Tone – is a general term to describe a tint or shade.

- Complementary colours – pairs of colours that appear on opposite sides of the colour wheel; for example red and green, or blue and orange.

Descriptive names for colours are often taken from nature, for example from:

- Flowers – violet, rose, lilac
- Food – cherry, lime, chocolate, olive
- Insects- vermilion and carmine
- Precious stones – emerald, ruby, cornelian
- Minerals – gold, rust, cobalt, terracotta
- Fish – salmon
- Places – Magenta, Sienna

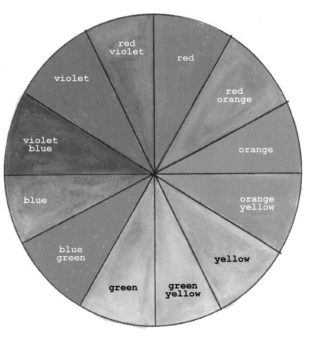

Design Process – Colour

Cultural differences affect the way in which we view and wear colours; these appear differently on varying skin colours and in different intensities of light. Diana Vreeland's famous quote that 'Pink is the navy blue of India' is an example of this.

In viewing a design, colour often has an overriding visual impact over other design considerations. A garment's message can be completely altered by the colour; for example, a severe cut can be softened if it is executed in a candy pink.

Colour takes on symbolism and often indicates mood. Mood is affected by situation, place, time and wearer; for example, black is often seen as a safe colour but perhaps not for a wedding dress.

Most designers don't choose their colour schemes with theory in mind. The fabrics selected will already have been created in the forthcoming season's colours. Designers use their skill in interpreting the colour palettes presented at fabric fairs and from their knowledge of the target customer and previous season's sales. There is also a gut feeling here for what creates a pleasing effect.

Colours can warm up, cool down, make practical or impractical, create impact or camouflage. There are certain shades of black, brown, camel, grey and blue, based on natural colour schemes, that are easy to wear; these create the basics of most people's wardrobe. Other colour schemes follow fashion in a more cyclical manner depending on the current vogue or market area.

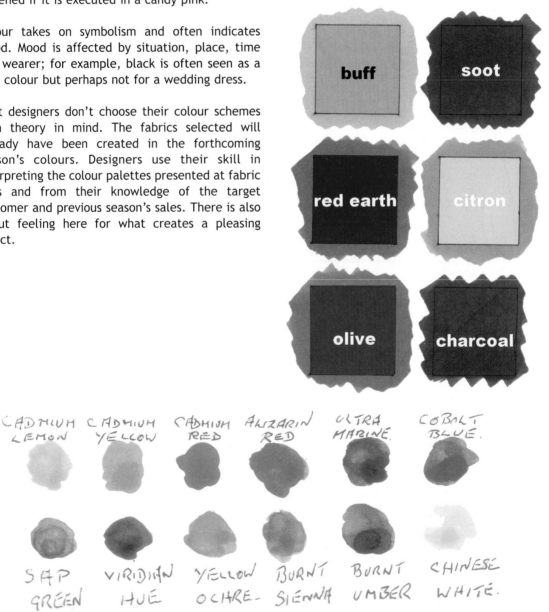

43

Design Process – Colour

Achromatic schemes are colourless, black, white and grey.

Monochromatic schemes are based on shades of the same colour.

Complementary schemes combine shades from the opposite ends of the colour wheel.

Design Process – Silhouette

Memorable works of art have memorable silhouettes, whether they are architectural, sculptural, painting, or by analogy, literature and music. In fashion design the term silhouette refers to the overall shape and volume of the design. During the 20th century, fashion designers experimented with volume and form creating silhouettes that forged a meaningful relationship between the garment and the body; some have become synonymous with particular forms such as Christian Dior's A-line.

The scanning of a mass involves two activities, namely exploration of the perimeter and area of volume forming a silhouette, whilst the content reveals the inner space and relates to proportion within. Silhouette can change dramatically but is often one of the more constant factors in fashion that evolves slowly, over a period of time.

Developing the silhouette is one of the most important design considerations and one that is easy to overlook when working on paper in a two-dimensional context. Mistakes or lack of thought here have repercussions when the design is taken into the prototype stage (see Design Development). Consider your designs as shapes that have a front, back and side view. How does the overall shape relate to the human form?

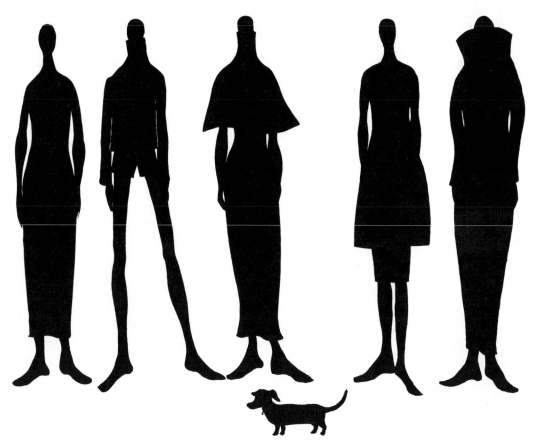

During the history of fashion there have been extreme shapes created for and around the human body, forcing changes in the desirable silhouette; these are often associated with the social, political and economic influences of the time. Relationships can be seen in the dominant forms of a particular era; for example, the tall points of gothic architecture are echoed in the high hats and pointed shoes of the same period. There is a similarity in the flat, broad style of Tudor architecture and the broad shoes and hats of that time. Often silhouettes are referred to by symbols that they resemble, for example a barrel or a bell.

Design Process – Silhouette

Soft A-line

Square-shouldered
rectangular shape

A-line silhouette

I-line silhouette

This silhouette is only visible
from the side or rear view

Silhouette created by
accessories

Two silhouettes that divide the body into
distinct sections

Design Process – Silhouette

Barrel-shaped coat

Headwear creates the silhouette

The V-line silhouette

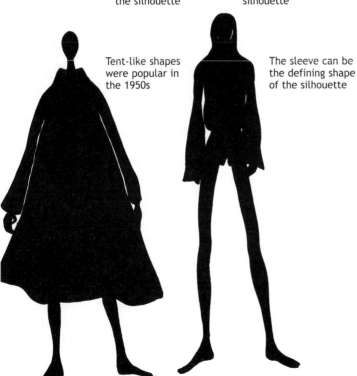

Hour-glass silhouette

High-waisted empire line

Tent-like shapes were popular in the 1950s

The sleeve can be the defining shape of the silhouette

The balloon skirt

Design Process – Silhouette

REVOLUTION OR EVOLUTION?

Silhouettes often remain the same for a period of time or evolve slowly, then they suddenly undertake a dramatic change. The reason for this is often complex but is based on the underlying social and cultural events of the time.

The garments and silhouettes illustrated here provide an example of how body shape can be radically changed, although most of these are now only considered within a historical or costume context. Many have been revived in recent years.

The great designers of the 19th and 20th century were influential in creating silhouettes that forged new directions in fashion design. Charles Frederick Worth introduced the tunic dress in 1860 and in 1870 introduced the bustle which superseded the crinoline. He is noted for introducing a more simple line and removing excessive frills and ruffles. Coco Chanel from 1912 innovated a modern, sporty way of dressing. He popularised the loose chemise, suits, yachting pants, blazers and knitwear, in sharp contrast to the costumes of the pre World War II period. Madeleine Vionnet was influential from the 1930s for introducing simple fluid shapes closely moulded to the body line using bias cutting, and was also known for cowl and halter necklines.

The blouson is a hip length jacket or blouse with fullness gathered below the waist giving a wider silhouette at or below the hip. The style originates from the anorak worn by Inuit people.

The bustle is a pad made of various materials attached to the back below the waist. Popular in the 1860s and 1870s also by Comme de Garçons and Vivienne Westwood during the 1980s.

The S-bend silhouette became fashionable towards the end of the 19th century. It was achieved by wearing a restrictive corset which produced a heavy over-hanging mono-bosom. This was balanced by a projecting behind created by a padded bustle and flowing skirts.

The poncho was cut from a square-shaped piece of fabric with a head opening and originated in South America.

Design Process – Silhouette

Cristobal Balenciaga created elegant and dramatic silhouettes that were often stark and formal. In 1939 he developed a dropped shoulder line, nipped in waist, and rounded hip line. In 1956 he created a new look by raising hemlines in front and dropping them behind.

Pierre Balmain popularised bell-shaped skirts in 1945. He created slender elegant lines and designed more sporty lines for the American market. He is noted for sheath dresses and capes.

Christian Dior's 'New Look' of 1947 featured tiny waists and boned bodices; the huge skirts could use up to 20 metres of fabric. The feminine look was in contrast to the utilitarian war years. The H-line introduced in 1954, pushed up the bust and dropped the waist to hip level making the crossbar of the letter H. His sack silhouette of 1957, a loose chemise shape, created a blueprint for a more relaxed and modern way of dressing.

Yves Saint Laurent was hugely influential in creating the modern silhouette, particularly in adapting traditional menswear styles into womenswear – trouser suits, smoking jackets and overcoats. His 'trapeze' line of 1958 created a narrow-shouldered, fitted bodice and full skirt that influenced the silhouette of the early 1960s.

During the 1970s and 1980s Rei Kawakubo pioneered non-traditional clothing, creating new silhouettes by experimenting with draping and volume that does not relate to the body in an accepted manner.

The hobble skirt, made popular by Poiret, created a 'V' silhouette by having its narrowest section from knees to ankle, allowing only the smallest of steps to be taken by the wearer.

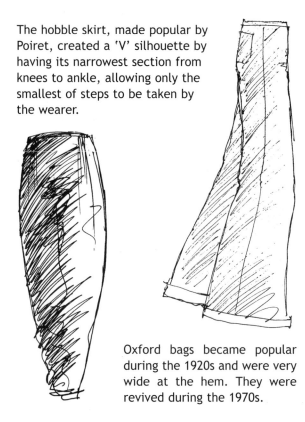

The beehive was a hairstyle popular in the late 1950s. Hair was severely back-combed to create a tall domed effect.

Oxford bags became popular during the 1920s and were very wide at the hem. They were revived during the 1970s.

Bubble shapes became popular during the 1950s as cocktail wear. Givenchy and Yves Saint Laurent were notable for developing these silhouettes.

The parka is a hooded garment with a long and loose silhouette. The 'snorkel' parka gave the head a periscope shape.

Design Process – Silhouette

Illustrated here are some examples of 20th century silhouettes. They represent a 'look' that was popular during each decade, where often a number of silhouettes could be fashionable simultaneously.

In general terms the 1920s saw a rise in hemlines and a flattening of the curved feminine shape, popular at the turn of the century. A boy-like figure was admired and hair was cut short with hats closely fitted to the head in contrast to the large bedecked hats of the Edwardian era.

The 1930s saw a more feminine shape return with a longer length and rounder figure. Hollywood influenced dress design and popularised cosmetics. Shoes got higher heels. Mass production began to influence design as zips and new fabrics started to emerge. Bias cutting achieved a close fit to the body in evening wear and the back became the focus of attention. The silhouette of World War II was necessarily utilitarian and had a square-shouldered, tailored line. Cloth rationing kept designs neat.

1920s   1930s   1940s   1950s

Design Process – Silhouette

Developments in textile technology created materials that had new capabilities. This initiated experimentation with unusual sculptural shapes from the 1950s. Expert cutting and construction techniques were utilised in order to create the silhouettes that maximised the impact of scale and volume. The hips were the focus of attention and shapes were created to emphasise this feature.

The transition to the 1960s saw one of the biggest changes as women adopted A-line child-like shapes, mini skirts and trousers. Designers experimented with new materials and futuristic silhouettes, and were increasingly influenced by historical and ethnic shapes. The trouser silhouette inverted from the 1950s' capri and 'slack' styles into flares and bell bottoms which continued well into the 1970s. Silhouettes and hairstyles were geometric.

1950s   1950s   1960s

Design Process – Silhouette

Towards the end of the 1960s hemlines dropped to 'midi' or 'maxi' lengths as a new romantic look became fashionable. A nostalgic mood prevailed with a revival of the 1930s style and the Victorian and Edwardian period popularised by Biba and Laura Ashley, retrospectively. During the mid-1970s trousers became straighter, skirts returned to the knee, and soft tailored shapes and blousons created a natural silhouette. The early 1980s featured nautical and romantic styles and the appropriation of sportswear into daywear created a new body-conscious silhouette. The silhouette of the mid-1980s changed into a 'V', as square-shouldered 'power' dressing dominated.

Trousers were adopted by women during World War II but were considered to be for utility purposes only. Although trousers became more popular during the 1950s and 1960s they did not become acceptable for workwear until the mid-1970s. For some professions and occasions they are still considered unacceptable.

During the second half of the 20th century a more pluralistic form of dressing had emerged and individuals throughout the 1980s and 1990s continued to create their own looks from modern styles forged from new developments in fabric technology, ethnic, and retro sources.

1960s   1970s   1980s

Design Process – Silhouette

DESIGNING WITH SILHOUETTES

When designing a collection it is important to develop the silhouette; try drawing this from all angles – front, back and side views. Draw loose shapes around the human form and experiment with scale and volume. Try exaggerating the focal points; are they the collar or the sleeves? Experiment with the stance of your model, the attitude of the wearer is an important part of contemporary style.

Spatial reasoning is a skill that can be developed. Experiment with proportions using combinations of scale, volume, colour, fabric, and shape before progressing to style lines or surface decoration. Think architecturally, build your silhouette, experiment with proportion, design the fit and structure and finally decorate and trim.

Design Process – Proportion

PROPORTION AND DESIGN

Proportion refers to the linear sub-division of objects and shapes, and concerns the balance of shape, volume, colour, fabric, texture and scale. The combination of these elements makes the design of garments infinitely diverse.

Having a 'sense of proportion' can be said to be subjective, in that the divisions in shapes can appear to be 'right' or 'wrong' depending on personal view and contemporary values. However, many theories have been expounded on the possibility of mathematical rules, which would provide a formula for perfect and pleasing harmonies, like the golden mean (see page 55). Historically proportion is sometimes rationalised, for example the classical line during the Renaissance.

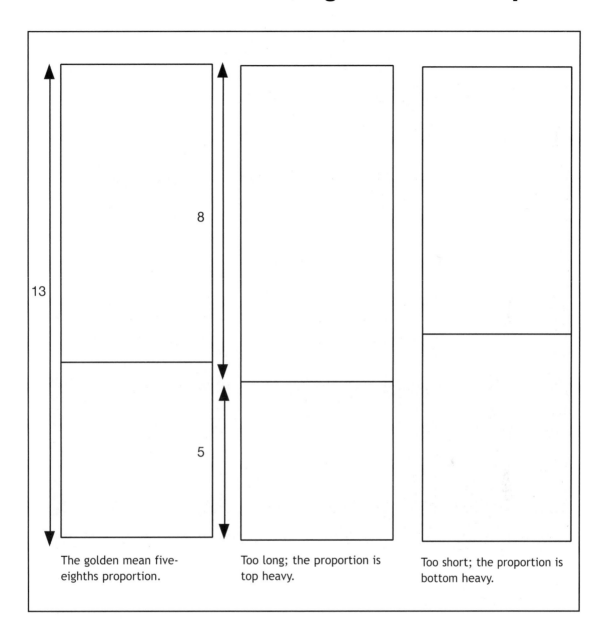

13 8 5		
The golden mean five-eighths proportion.	Too long; the proportion is top heavy.	Too short; the proportion is bottom heavy.

THE GOLDEN MEAN

The golden mean was developed by taking actual measurements of ancient sculpture where it was found that a 5 : 8 proportional relationship usually existed between the sections of which these figures were composed. There is a general consensus that these proportions are also pleasing when applied to the visual arts and garment design.

These classical proportions are not always fashionable; 'out-of-proportion' styles have been equally popular. Fashion flips between the orthodox and traditional and the alternative and challenging; because of this the golden mean should not be adopted as an absolute rule.

Design Process – Proportion

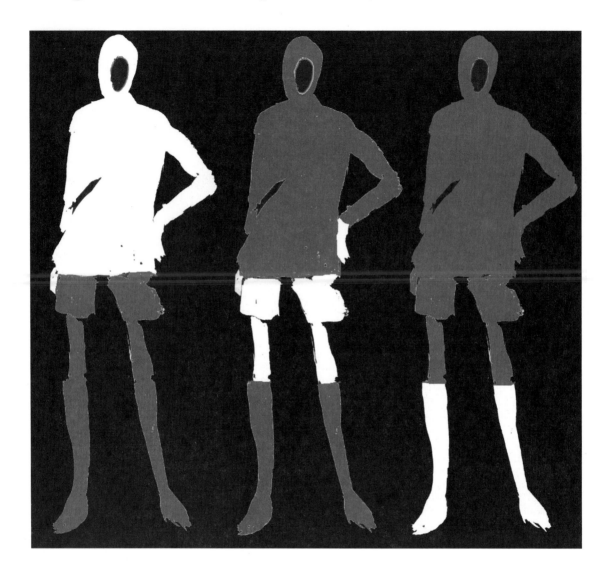

BALANCE

A simple silhouette of a sporty hooded top, shorts and boots can look dramatically different with proportionate colour effects. Filling large areas with contrasting shades is known as colour blocking. A garment achieves balance from the relative volume and size of the style lines and details used in its design. It only becomes successful when it satisfies the eye in terms of its balance. This sense of balance is based on a complex range of comparisons relating to both a classic sense of what is a pleasing proportion (see The Golden Mean) and whatever the contemporary view of proportional scale happens to be.

The sense of proportion in a garment has to be exacting, it is critical to achieve exactly the right lines for seams, size of collar or position of pocket; this is closely linked to human scale and shape. Every era has its own ideal body shape, and as this changes so does our sense of garment proportion.

Colour blocking a simple outfit demonstrates a few of the many combinations possible and their varying effects.

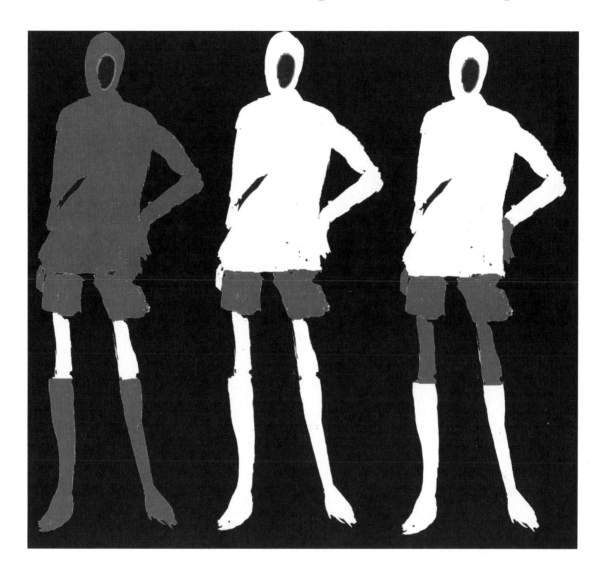

POSITIVE AND NEGATIVE

Using positive and negative effects in colour blocking is a good design development exercise where dramatic differences in balance and proportion can be achieved. A positive creates a negative and vice versa and these elements create rhythm when repeated. An optical 'dazzling' effect can be created when the two elements are used in equal measure or too closely together. Positive and negative act as a separator, creating maximum visual impact and can be used not only for colour contrast but for hard and soft, coarse and smooth, solid and void, pattern and plain.

The designer can use this powerful tool in order to focus attention on or away from a feature of the design or the figure.

Design Process – Proportion

Artistic balance can be divided into two types: symmetrical and asymmetrical. Symmetry is achieved by an equal distribution from the centre of impact and equal volume. Asymmetry can be achieved in three ways: by equal volume and unequal impact, by unequal volume and equal impact, or by unequal volume and unequal impact.

The more elements that are contained in the design, the more difficult it is to achieve a pleasing, balanced end result.

Equal volume and unequal impact

Design Process – Proportion

Unequal volume and
unequal impact

Unequal volume and equal impact

Design Process – Proportion

SCALE

The term scale is used to express the relationship between a garment and its design details. The eye tends to determine size and relevant scale in relation to the silhouette of the garment and its wearer. Design elements need to harmonise within the total design and not be out of scale, for example too large or too small, too bright or too dark.

RHYTHM

The use of rhythm as a design tool is important in achieving pleasing effects. Rhythm in design results from lines and masses that form repetitions; these repetitions can be either uniform or of decreasing or increasing size. Rhythmic patterns can be generated by superimposing scales.

The examples here demonstrate the effects of scale using simple patterns of floral, circle, square, stripe and mesh. There are a number of design considerations in using scale to create impact. In utilising large-scale patterns it is important to consider where the overall repeat or single motifs will fall in relation to the body shape, fastenings and seam construction. Heavily patterned, textured or elaborate fabrics are best made up in simple designs. Smaller-scale patterns are easier to work with and can be combined, so in these examples light and dark, and scale, have been used to create impact.

Design Process – Proportion

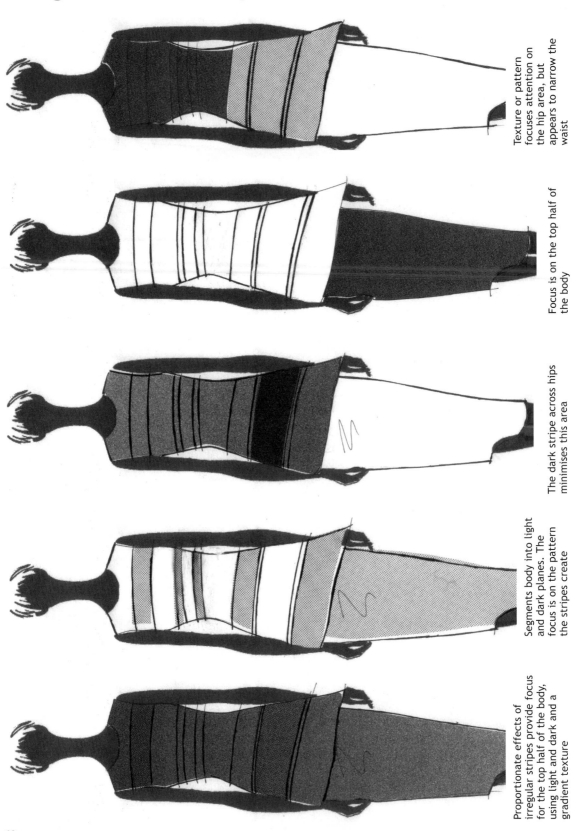

Texture or pattern focuses attention on the hip area, but appears to narrow the waist

Focus is on the top half of the body

The dark stripe across hips minimises this area

Segments body into light and dark planes. The focus is on the pattern the stripes create

Proportionate effects of irregular stripes provide focus for the top half of the body, using light and dark and a gradient texture

Design Process – Proportion

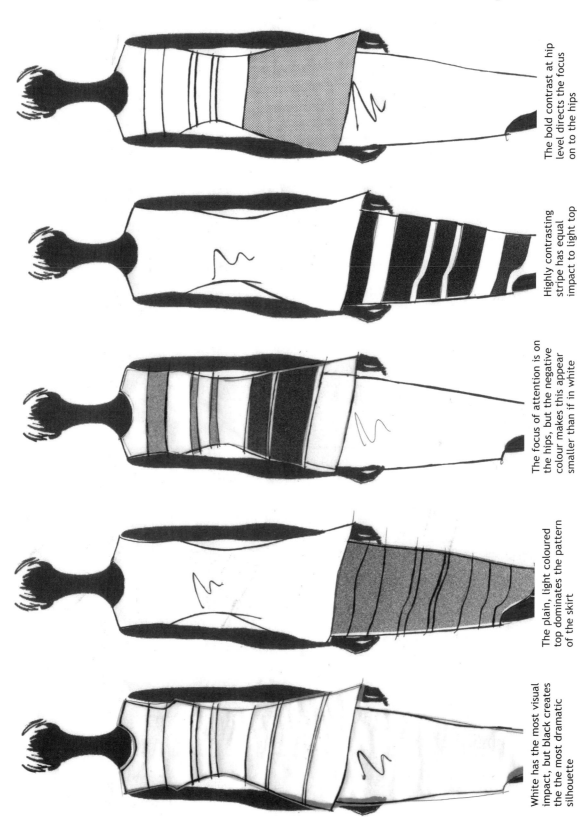

The bold contrast at hip level directs the focus on to the hips

Highly contrasting stripe has equal impact to light top

The focus of attention is on the hips, but the negative colour makes this appear smaller than if in white

The plain, light coloured top dominates the pattern of the skirt

White has the most visual impact, but black creates the the most dramatic silhouette

Design Process – Understanding Fabric

INTRODUCTION TO FABRIC

Designers working in mass production have to be able to translate their two-dimensional designs into three-dimensional garments. It may take years to develop experience of fabric properties and how to best exploit their characteristics. This section intends to introduce the prospective designer to the visual, tactile and structural qualities of fabrics, their texture and pattern.

It is important to have a background knowledge of fabric construction and technical performance. Most successful designs utilise the best qualities of the materials from which they are constructed.

With the selected fabrics the designer will cut swatches in order to try out combinations and create fabric stories that will eventually form the range.

From here the designer usually makes samples of interesting finishes, edges, stitch details and other processes in order to experiment with the fabric and discover its potential.

Any interesting ideas that develop from this experimentation can then be incorporated into the design drawings.

CUT SWATCHES

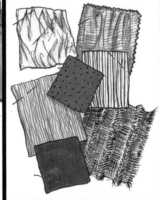

Draping qualities and fabric behaviour, for example flimsy, fluid, bulky, lank

Design Process – Understanding Fabric

FABRIC BEHAVIOUR

It is important to become familiar with the behaviour of fabrics. Sampling in different fabrics helps to broaden the designer's experience. Different fabrics require different finishes. For example a faux fur fabric, with a long pile, requires quite a different treatment to a transparent fabric where all seams and finishes will be visible.

Tweed coat   Microfibre coat

Faux fur coat   PVC coat

Fabrics are often referred to by their handling properties:

- Dry – crêpes, micros, bouclés.
- Crispy, with a papery feel – poplins, taffetas, organdies, organzas.
- Slippery – satins, silks, cupro.
- Soapy – peach bloom.
- Rubberised – talc-like whitish coating, neoprene, foam.
- Oily – waxed cottons.
- Glazed, varnished, lacquered – nylons, coated.
- Plush – velvets, chenilles, velours, dévoré, fleece.
- Fluid – fine jersey, chiffons, georgettes, silks.
- Polished – mercerised cotton.
- Bonded – foam backed onto another fabric.
- Stiff – denim, drills.
- Felted – wool, blanket-like.
- Brushed – mohair.

The same garment design made in different fabrics will create different effects. The handle refers to how it feels to the hand – rough, smooth, warm, cool.

In the illustrations on this page, the PVC coat is stiff, light and cool whilst the tweed is thick, heavy and warm. The microfibre has draping qualities whilst the faux fur has none. Note the change in silhouette from lean (microfibre) to the rounded (faux fur).

The fabric composition and its weave, knit or bonding method determines its texture and handle. Texture plays an important role in clothing; it is its tactile qualities that make a garment sensual to the touch. What we wear next to our skin and how it might feel is an important factor in the success of a design.

Design Process – Understanding Fabric

Fabric is the tool with which a fashion designer creates. The fabric dictates the cut, drape and silhouette of a garment, but the fibre dictates the performance and behaviour of the fabric. There are many points to consider when designing with fabric to ensure that it is fit for the purpose intended.

What is important to the designer is not the chemical composition but the fabric's aesthetic appearance, handle, drape and structure in addition to the design restrictions of the market area and season.

The designer can become a specialist in a particular field by experimenting with specific types of fabric season after season. He/she will often establish their reputation and 'signature style' upon their knowledge and use of certain fabrics.

Points to consider about a fabric:

- **Weight** – will determine the 'drape' or 'hang' of a garment.
- **Weave** – the drape again must be considered, but also the manufacturing; for example with an open weave hems and interfacing will be visible. Is a lining required?
- **Texture** – soft, smooth textures are attractive but rougher fabrications can be also – this depends on the look that is desired.
- **Colour** – does it work with accents, contrasts, blocks, print, pattern?
- **Width** – depending on the size of the pattern pieces, the width of a fabric is a very important consideration (to avoid unnecessary or non-desired seaming).
- **Price** – some fibres are cheaper than others and pricing of a garment needs to remain competitive. However, these days all types of natural and synthetic fibres are mixed together to achieve different types of performance.

FABRIC TYPES

Wovens: Produced on a loom using warp and weft yarns. The warp is placed long ways and parallel in the loom, the weft yarn is carried across the loom from side to side and passed over and under the warp. A variety of weaves are possible, for example plain, hopsack, satin, twill, herringbone and chevron, rib, jacquard, dobby, leno.

Knits and jerseys: One continuous yarn or a number of continuous yarns are used; yarns are looped together to form a 'mesh'. Knitted fabrics have more elastic properties than woven ones. A variety of knits are possible – warp knit, weft knit or filling knits, sliver knitting. Jersey is a tubular weft or filling knit fabric made with a plain stitch. Double jersey is a firmer fabric with less give, made using two sets of latched needles, cut edges do not curl up and garments have a firmer hang.

Non-woven fabrics: A sheet structure made from fibres held together by mechanical, chemical, thermal or solvent means or a combination of these.

Design Process – Understanding Fabric

Lace: Machine-made lace is manufactured on a net base on which patterns are embroidered. 'Schiffli' embroidery imitates hand-embroidered lace on a plain net. If the background is burnt out or dissolved 'guipure' lace is the result. If embroidery is applied to plain weave cotton then broderie anglaise or eyeletting is the result.

Net: A mesh produced by twisting two sets of bobbins.

FABRIC FINISHES

Sanding: Mechanical abrading is used whereby the fabric is passed, dry, over a series of rollers covered with emery paper which rub and break the fibres to produce a soft weathered effect. Also known as emerised, sueded (for heavier fabric types) or peau de pêche (suede-like fabrics are not achieved in this way). The process removes shine and softens the handle and colour.

Washing: Sandwashing, like stonewashing, uses the abrasive power of mineral particles in the wash. Being finer, it is generally applied to silk and viscose fabrics and has a similar effect to using sandpaper.

Mercerising: Mercerising is a shrinkage process which involves passing fabric through a cold solution of 15–20% sodium carbonate, causing the flat ribbon-like cotton fibres to swell in cross-section and contract in length, making it much more lustrous. The process increases strength by as much as 20% and makes the fibres more receptive to dyes.

Coating: The earliest 'performance' fabrics were wovens coated with natural oils or wax to keep out water. Increasingly, though, with the benefits of petrochemical technology, the base fabric is used only to act as a stable ground for a layer of plastic. Many of what are called coated fabrics are little more than the coated layer itself. These fabrics are often finished by 'embossing' to give animal skin effects, created much like pile embossing. Polyurethane and polyvinyl chloride (PVC) are the most common materials. Companies are reluctant to divulge

details of the different chemical treatments that create high gloss, matt or metallic finishes.

Glazing: Starch, shellac or glue can be applied to the surface of a fabric to give a glazed or polished appearance. The surface is then ironed under pressure. The finish allows resistance to dirt penetration and is often applied to cotton fabrics making them stiff and shiny.

Burn-out: The fabric is made from two fibres, for example polyester and cotton. A pattern effect is achieved by using a screen to force through chemicals which burn away one of the fibres, leaving sheer and opaque areas.

Anti-bacterial: Fabrics can acquire a self-sterilising quality by applying an antiseptic finish. The fabric remains unaffected by perspiration and can be washed or dry cleaned.

There are many more finishes possible which come and go with the vagaries of fashion; this is not a definitive list.

Design Process – Understanding Fabric

Fabrics are further classified by their composition and can be divided into:

- **Animal** – derived from an animal source.
- **Vegetable** – derived from a plant.
- **Natural polymer** fibre produced by man from a naturally occurring polymeric substance.
- **Man-made** fibre that has been created from a chemical structure.

ANIMAL

- Alpaca
- Angora - Angora rabbit
- Camel hair – Bactrian camel
- Cashgora – Cashgora goat
- Cashmere – Cashmere goat
- Guanaco – guanaco
- Horsehair
- Llama
- Mohair- Angora goat
- Silk
- Vicuna
- Wool

VEGETABLE

- Coir
- Cotton
- Flax
- Hemp
- Jute
- Kapok
- Linen
- Pina
- Raffia
- Ramie
- Sisal

MAN-MADE

- Acrylic
- Aramid
- Elastane
- Modacrylic
- Nylon
- Polyacrylonitrile
- Polyamide
- Polyester
- Polyethylene
- Polypropylene
- Polytetrafluoroethylene
- Polyurethane
- Polyvinyl chloride (PVC)
- Vinyl

NATURAL POLYMERS

- Acetate
- Cupro™
- Elastodiene
- Metal fibre
- Modal™
- Lyocell
- Triacetate
- Viscose
- Tencel™

NEW DEVELOPMENTS

It is important to be aware of technological developments when designing so that the best and most relevant fabrics may be used for the job. Consumers are demanding qualities from textiles that will enhance their lifestyle such as: comfort, performance, fit, shape retention, trans-seasonal versatility, quality and style, added value, lightweight properties and ecological integrity.

The consumer will continue spending where they see innovation. There are many forward-thinking ideas in fibre and fabric manufacturing. There follows a range of fibre and fabric areas under development.

Design Process – Understanding Fabric

NEW DEVELOPMENTS IN TRADITIONAL FIBRES

- The growing of already coloured cotton.
- Organically produced, water repellant, waxed cotton.
- Compatible, shrink resistance between wool and cotton or cotton and cashmere.
- Non-iron or stain-resistant finishes applied to cotton and linen.

NON-TRADITIONAL FIBRE SOURCES

- It is possible to blend **jute** with other fibres for strength.
- **Nettle** provides a fine, strong yarn and has good insulation properties.
- **Hemp** is a soft but strong fibre.
- **Sisal** has good antistatic properties and can be blended with other fibres.
- **Pineapple** and **banana leaves** provide a silk-like fibre but they are expensive to produce.
- **Peat** fibres produce a felt-like fabric with good antistatic, hypoallergenic and absorbent properties.
- **Alginate** is used for dressings and promotes healing. It is water soluble and flame resistant.

SYNTHETIC POLYMERS

- Polypropylene, traditionally used in packaging and sacking, produces a strong, fine, waterproof fabric with good thermal properties.
- Polyethylene, traditionally used for banners and packaging, can be used for disposable fashion items.

- Polyvinyl chloride (PVC) is used for finishing and coating textiles and can be heat set for interesting creations as it is heat sensitive.

OTHER MATERIALS

Metals: Steel, copper and aluminium can be used in knitted, woven and non-woven fabrics.

Rubber: Fine latex can now be used for garments and accessories. It can also be moulded to create seamless shapes.

Paper: There is development work in using paper for textiles; they may have a polyurethane coating and have high strength, good light fastness and temperature resistance.

Glass: Fibres can be included into textiles for reflective purposes, but have poor abrasion qualities.

Ceramic: Used with polyester, ceramic fibres can offer waterproof qualities and ultra-violent (UV) protection and can help to maintain body temperatures when incorporated into textiles.

BLENDING

Silk and steel: Silky yarns mixed with steel can produce fine but firm constructions.

Wool: Wool may be blended with other fibres, such as Kevlar™ (bullet-proof fabric) to produce a more robust, textural, performance fabric.

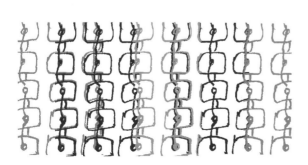

Design Process – Understanding Fabric

Fabrics are becoming 'smarter' and performance characteristics are being embedded into textiles during construction, making the development of fibre and fabric as significant as the cut and shape of the garment itself.

Basic principles can produce stunning results such as the thermoplastic qualities of synthetic fabrics – creases and pleats and other shapes can be permanently 'set' by subjecting the fabric to heat. Once the shape is 'locked' in it will remain for the life of the garment.

There are new terms used with regard to textile development such as 'performance', 'high performance', 'technical', 'intelligent' and 'smart'. They are used on a regular basis to describe fabrics that possess certain character-istics, such as breathability, anti-bacterial or ultra-violet (UV) ray protection.

Protection is important in textile development and bullet-proof fabrics offer this. There is a fabric called 'No Violence™', which is said to be five times stronger than steel and is impervious to knives and bullets, yet it looks and feels like cashmere. Many new developments can be sourced from NASA and the Ministry of Defence, the latter having discovered 'plasma processing', a technique by which garments can be kept stain and dirt resistant. It is predicted that we will be using self-mending and self-cleaning fabrics with those that protect us from electromagnetic waves.

There are crossovers between what is performance and what is smart. Fabrics that change colour in response to heat and light correspond with the abilities that we associate with smart materials; they begin to protect us and even make decisions for us. Smart materials have the ability to be:

- Programmed to adapt to various condi-tions and react to the environment.
- Possess all the qualities traditionally required in a fabric and others not anticipated.
- Responsive and customising to our form each time they are worn.

Recent research offers fabrics with responsive films and gels which alter their fluid characteristics and become rigid in the event of a fall. Further military developments from the United States government have led to tests on garments which track soldiers so that command centre recognises when a soldier is injured, even determining the severity of the injury. These techniques could be invaluable if applied to children's apparel.

Textiles can respond to the environment; some can sense when it is raining and the holes between the fibres and stitches will close up and protect the wearer from the rain.

Perhaps the smartest fabrics could include the use of microchip and semi-conductor technology implanted into fibres which act as 24-hour monitors. Information could be stored or transferred between individuals through the use of microchips in garments or footwear.

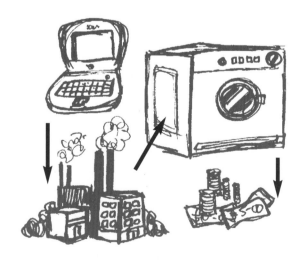

Design Process – Understanding Fabric

Visuals derived from Philips Electronics NV
Research Website

Research presently being carried out using electro-textiles, these being conductive textiles which perform a range of basic electronic functions, has resulted in an 'intelligent' waistcoat that could give disabled children the power of 'speech' when linked to a speech synthesiser.

Wearable mechanisms are now being developed which allow us to protect ourselves and adapt to changes in the environment. Daniel Cooper has designed a 'chameleon jacket' that monitors and protects wearers from pollution. The jacket can be worn in a 'passive' or an 'aggressive' state depending upon pollution levels. Built-in detectors change from blue where there is little or no pollution to orange for serious pollution levels.

Aesthetic effects such as holographic finishes have been pioneered by such designers as Issey Miyake. His jacket and trouser designs were made from monofilament polyamide with a holographic finish applied.

Fibre optics are widely used in fine art installations. Designers such as American Sonja Flavin use fibre optics interlaced with Lucite™, the trade name for a sheet of plastic which can be cast, extruded and manipulated. Garments made using the integration of fibre optics and regular fibres means that television waves can be received at leisure, allowing the wearer to watch television programmes from their garments.

A revolutionary new hi-tech, light-reflecting fabric from swimwear manufacturers, Speedo, is claimed to make white swimsuits stay opaque when wet. Water repellent or 'hydrophobic' fabric may be used to make the thinnest, strongest, most waterproof coats ever.

Kevlar™ can be made into a convincing leather-look fabric called Keprotec™, which is windproof, waterproof, breathable, bulletproof and almost indestructible even when set on fire.

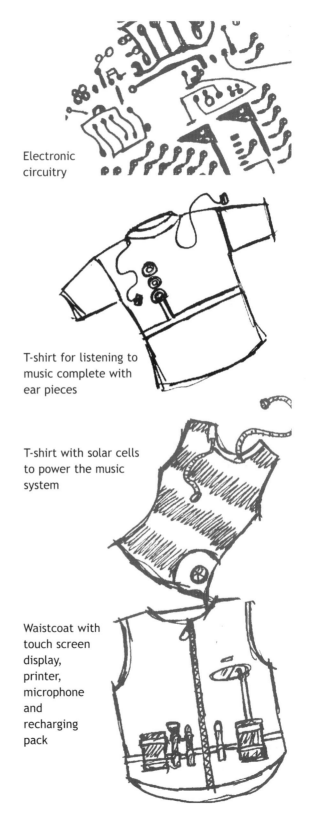

Electronic circuitry

T-shirt for listening to music complete with ear pieces

T-shirt with solar cells to power the music system

Waistcoat with touch screen display, printer, microphone and recharging pack

Design Process – Understanding Fabric

Visuals derived from Philips Electronics NV Research Website

This ski jacket has a microphone to enable contact with other skiers. There is a touch screen display for navigation purposes and a 'Help!' button to alert fellow skiers when in trouble.

Responsive textile products vary from the visually active, such as climbing a rope that changes colour under stress, to the visually passive such as the smart bra that regains its shape at certain temperatures during washing. These products are made from the same materials as their conventional counterparts with the addition of smart materials – for the rope a dye and for the bra shape memory alloys (SMAs). SMAs will return to their original shape after having been stressed.

The sportswear industry uses many performance fabrics before they filter through into more mainstream end uses. The dominance of sportswear has come about largely through the interest in health, fitness and sporting activities.

Medicines and vitamins are promoted in well-being products selling alongside sportswear products. Micro-encapsulation processes enable substances to be encapsulated into fibres and be slowly released to provide health benefits and promote healing.

Not only do these fabrics have technical ability, they also have deeper emotional, sensual qualities, providing the user with an extra psychological advantage. Research in Japan has shown that Tencel™ fabrics, manufactured by Acordis, have the capacity to improve the quality of life simply by making the wearer feel good by decreasing the negative waves which the brain emits during periods of stress.

SOME COMPANIES INVOLVED IN PRODUCTION OR AVAILABILITY OF NEW FABRIC DEVELOPMENTS

Acordis, Akzo Nobel, Alma, Carrington Performance, Cloth House, Cordura, DuPont, Dyneema, Ecospun, Enka Sun, Four D, Giovanni Crespi, Knitmesh, Konrad Hurnsch, Milior, Novaceta, Panotex, Perseverance Mills, Rhoyl'eco, Schoeller, Whaley's.

RESEARCHING NEW DEVELOPMENTS FOR NEW IDEAS

There are many more exciting developments and applications of textiles under way. What is driving the thought processes of researchers? How can designers maintain their *raison d'être* of 'form and function' and move forward into the future, with so much information available to them?

It is worth spending some of our precious time occasionally researching new developments. Awareness is important and having ideas is essential. Opportunities and experience allow for the investigation of ideas and concepts.

Design Process – Understanding Fabric

Colour always provides interest and impact. Printed and dyed textiles can attract consumers and convey new fashion trends easily and comparatively quickly. They help to balance collections or ranges and add variety. Some of the most common print and dyeing techniques are discussed here.

PRINTING TECHNIQUES

Block printing: This uses wooden blocks which are engraved with the design or the design is hammered into metal strips.

Burn-out printing: This is a technique whereby a chemical is printed on to a fabric constructed from two fibres. The chemical destroys one fibre creating sheer areas.

Discharge printing: A light pattern on a dark background is created by printing a paste on to the fabric. The paste removes the background colour.

Engraved roller printing: This uses images that are engraved on to a metal roller. The roller is inked and is transferred to the cloth under pressure.

Screen printing: Screen printing is based on the stencilling process. A fine mesh screen is created and the areas not to be printed are chemically blocked out by a photographic process. A different screen is needed for each colour required. A squeegee is used to push the printing ink through on to the cloth. This may be done by hand or by a machine, depending on whether the fabric is a sample length, a 'one-off' or for mass production. The textile may be printed before the garment is constructed or after depending on whether the print is a place print, a motif or a graphic print on cut pattern pieces.

Heat transfer printing: This works by passing a paper with the printed design through heated rollers, with the cloth, consequently transferring the print. Dye transfers from paper to cloth can be done by hand using coloured paper and a small heat press.

Printing inks: Glitter may be added to flat colour or hand-rendered paint effects. Flocking provides a velvety texture which depends upon the fibre used to flock. Expanding inks also provide texture and begin to expand after being applied to the cloth.

Photocopy transfer paper: This is a sampling or 'one-off' technique where a design may be photocopied on to a coated paper – the scale is limited to the scale of copies produced from the copier; a large print could be created by patching pieces together. The printed paper is then transferred to the cloth by heat, usually a heat press, sometimes an iron, depending upon the size of the print. The backing paper is then removed. This technique is useful for reproducing photographic quality imagery. If a design includes any text it is essential that this is reversed (as a mirror image) on the photocopier so that it will print the correct way round on the cloth.

Design Process – Understanding Fabric

Motif prints are a single figure distinct from the background of the fabric.

Repeat prints are one complete unit of the design that can be repeated in a number of ways across the fabric and upside down to allow for a variety of cutting techniques.

One-way prints can be expensive as they only allow the fabric to be cut from one direction.

Placed prints are applied when the garment has been constructed.

Logo prints are graphics treated like motif prints.

DYEING TECHNIQUES

Fabrics are either **yarn-dyed** or **piece-dyed**. Yarn-dyeing means that the yarns are coloured prior to weaving. They can be stored as raw yarn and dyed when required according to the dictates of fashion. Piece-dyeing means that cloth is woven as what is known as 'grey' goods and is then dyed according to fashion needs.

Direct dyeing requires only one immersion in colour and has no fixing process.

Disperse dyeing requires the fibre to be subjected to heat which makes it swell. The colour is then introduced under pressure.

Pigment dyes are mixed with a binding agent and applied to the fibre.

Basic, acid and naphthal dyes produce bright colours. Sulphur dyes have a limited colour range. Chrome dyes are used on wool with an additional chemical to aid penetration of the fibre.

Natural/vegetable dyes have been used traditionally for many years and often become fashionable because of their particular colour characteristics.

OTHER DYEING TECHNIQUES

Batik is native to Java. Molten wax is applied to the cloth in a hand-painting process. The wax hardens and provides a 'resist', the cloth is dyed and the process can be repeated over and over again to create more complex designs. The wax is removed to reveal a cracked wax, veined appearance. The background becomes progressively deeper with repeated dyeing.

Garment dyeing creates an over-dyed appearance on already constructed garments. The advantage of this process is that a combination of fabrics may have a similar tone of colour.

Ikat is a process whereby the yarns are 'space' dyed prior to weaving, producing a blurred effect. It is very popular, depending on fashion trends, and is a traditionally Oriental technique.

Ombré (shaded) is a technique whereby fabric is dyed with graduated tones from light to dark.

OTHER DECORATIVE EFFECTS

Embossing techniques use heat to produce permanent effects on thermoplastic fibres.

Crinkle can be achieved like embossing, by applying heated rollers to the fabric, or by applying caustic soda.

Puckering requires chemicals to be applied to the fabric which dissolve some fibres. When the cloth is drying these areas shrink, producing the pucker.

Moire can be achieved by impressing heated rollers on to, preferably, ribbed fabric. Light reflects on the processed ribbing to create a 'watery' effect.

Design Process – Understanding Fabric

Premiere Vision is the leading fabric trade fair in Europe, taking place at the Parc des Expositions in Paris biannually in early spring and early autumn. It is an extremely important forum for designers, buyers, manufacturers, marketers and academics to seek fabrics and fabric directions for their collections and research.

FABRIC TYPES

The show comprises three vast halls, broken down into forums, dedicated to covering: printed fabrics, knitwear, colour wovens/shirtings, wool-type fabrics/linens, silky aspects, top of the range silks, sportswear/activewear/denim and trimmings/lace/embroideries/textile accessories. Fabrics exhibited cover men's, women's and childrens-wear and some fabrics are suitable for all.

Inspiration and direction for the forum displays comes from professionals from all over Europe. These 59 members of the fashion industry offer their directional expertise, from prediction, fibre, yarn and fabric manufacture, to publishing and consultancy.

One hall of Premiere Vision is taken over by the audiovisual theatre, fibre exhibitors and fashion publication agencies. These agencies deal with two differing types of copy (see Research Direction – Fashion Prediction): fashion prediction books and fashion magazines. The former is a more specialist publication, issued 18 months to 2 years ahead and often accompanies personal consultancy given by the prediction company to the client.

AUDIOVISUAL PRESENTATION

Many visitors attend Premiere Vision for inspiration with regard to colour and fabric direction for the coming season. The 'audiovisual' trend presentation, packed with provoking imagery and sound, proves popular with all visitors.

THE FORUMS

The nine forums at the exhibition are dedicated to each of the eight fabric types and there is also a 'forum general'.

The forum displays are put together reflecting their fabric type with mood-evoking props which strengthen the general colours and fabric themes projected. The organisers pick fabrics from those manufacturers who they feel best represent their predicted themes and organise them according to colour to form a visually stimulating display. These presentations are useful to buyers and designers as they are able to reference the highlighted fabrics, and seek them out on their exhibitors' stands.

In hall two of the Parc des Expositions is Indigo, an exhibition for print designers which once was an integral part of Premiere Vision, but now, due to the number of exhibitors, has become a separate show and requires a separate entrance fee!

FABRIC AREAS

 LINEN

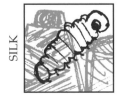 SILK

 COTTON

 MAN-MADE

 WOOL

 SYNTHETICS

 TRENDS

 INDEX

Design Process – Construction

The following pages discuss the basic techniques used to construct: basic skirts; basic bodices; skirts, panels and pleats; dresses; basic sleeves; basic trousers and basic collars. They show traditional methods of cutting woven cloth to achieve a method of creating a silhouette on the figure and are not intended to show contemporary fashion design. They do not include advanced cutting techniques or those for stretch woven or stretch knit fabrics, where the properties of those fabrics provide the necessary fit.

In order to begin designing it is important to understand the basic methods of fitting fabric to a bodyshape in order to achieve the desired silhouette and proportion. Consider the function of the design at this stage. How does it fasten?

Design Process – Construction – Basic Skirts

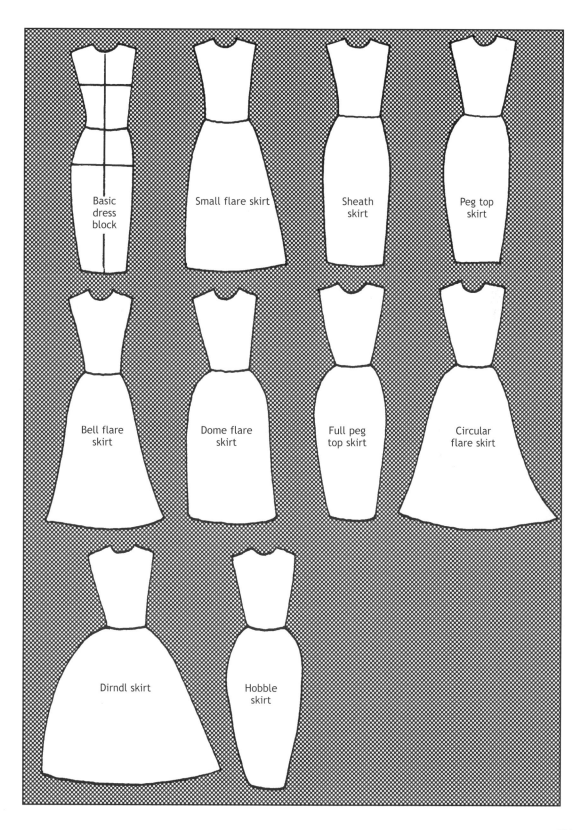

Basic dress block

Small flare skirt

Sheath skirt

Peg top skirt

Bell flare skirt

Dome flare skirt

Full peg top skirt

Circular flare skirt

Dirndl skirt

Hobble skirt

Design Process – Construction – Basic Bodices

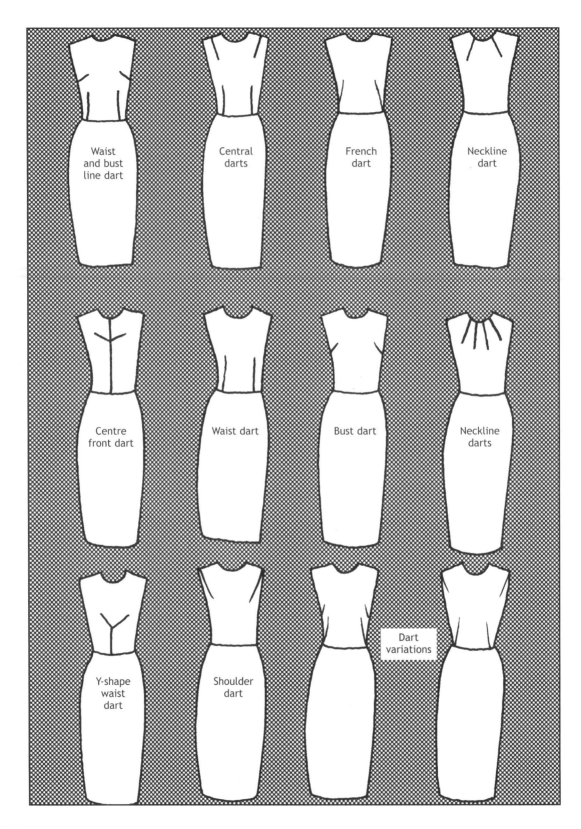

Waist and bust line dart

Central darts

French dart

Neckline dart

Centre front dart

Waist dart

Bust dart

Neckline darts

Y-shape waist dart

Shoulder dart

Dart variations

Design Process – Construction – Skirts/Panels

Gentle flare

A-line flare

A-line six gore

Medium flare

Four gore

Eight gore

Full flare

Semi-circular

Ten gore

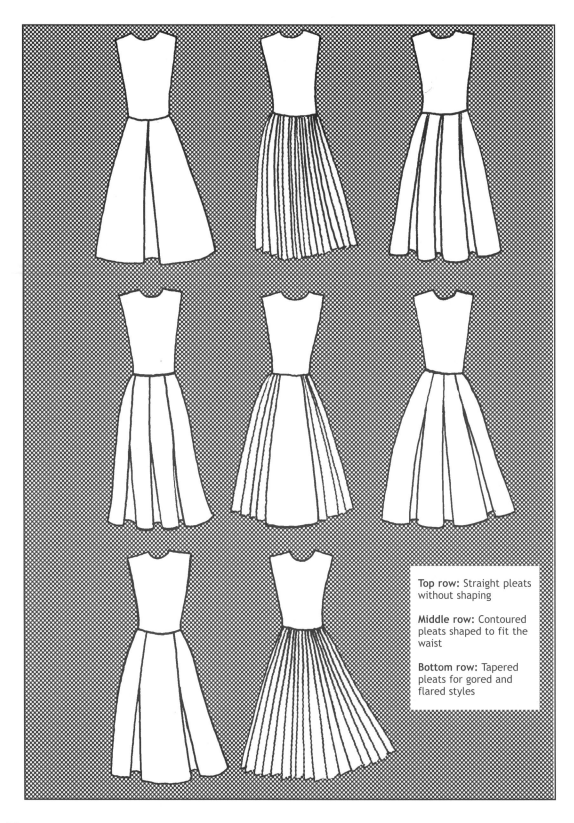

Top row: Straight pleats without shaping

Middle row: Contoured pleats shaped to fit the waist

Bottom row: Tapered pleats for gored and flared styles

Design Process – Construction – Dresses

Dresses constructed from bodices and skirts

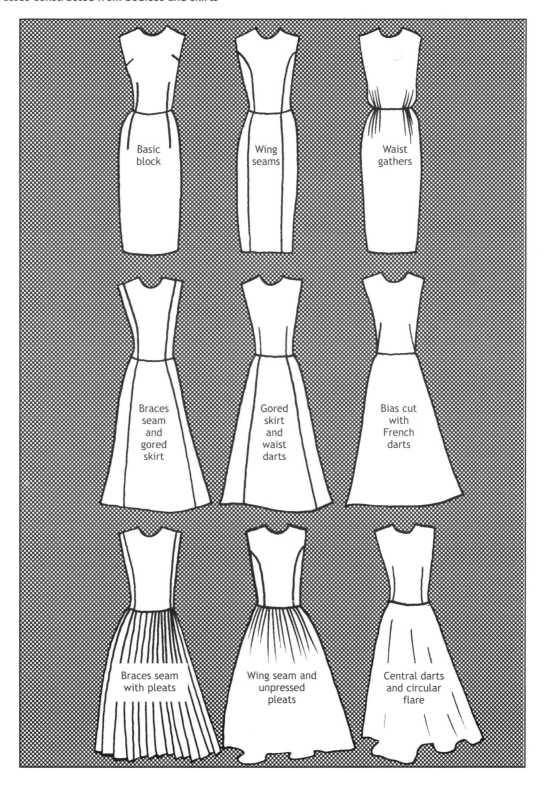

Basic block

Wing seams

Waist gathers

Braces seam and gored skirt

Gored skirt and waist darts

Bias cut with French darts

Braces seam with pleats

Wing seam and unpressed pleats

Central darts and circular flare

Design Process – Construction – Dresses

Dresses constructed in one piece

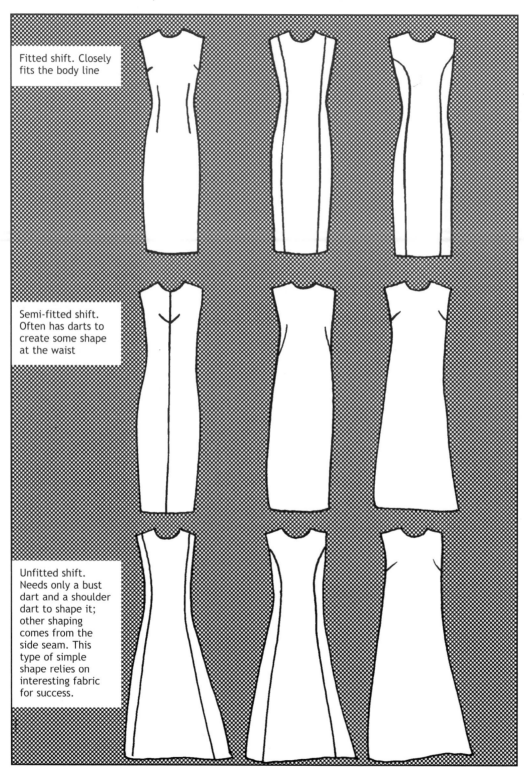

Fitted shift. Closely fits the body line

Semi-fitted shift. Often has darts to create some shape at the waist

Unfitted shift. Needs only a bust dart and a shoulder dart to shape it; other shaping comes from the side seam. This type of simple shape relies on interesting fabric for success.

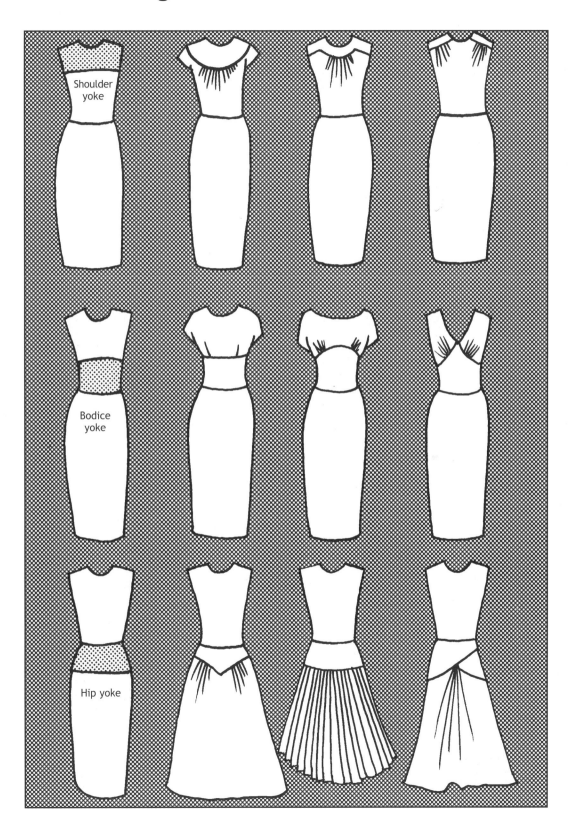

Shoulder yoke

Bodice yoke

Hip yoke

Design Process – Construction – Dresses

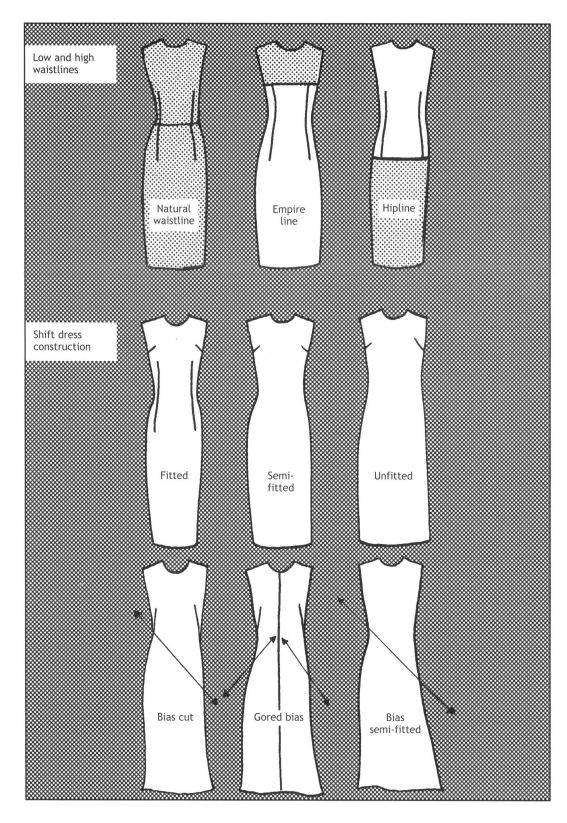

Low and high waistlines

Natural waistline

Empire line

Hipline

Shift dress construction

Fitted

Semi-fitted

Unfitted

Bias cut

Gored bias

Bias semi-fitted

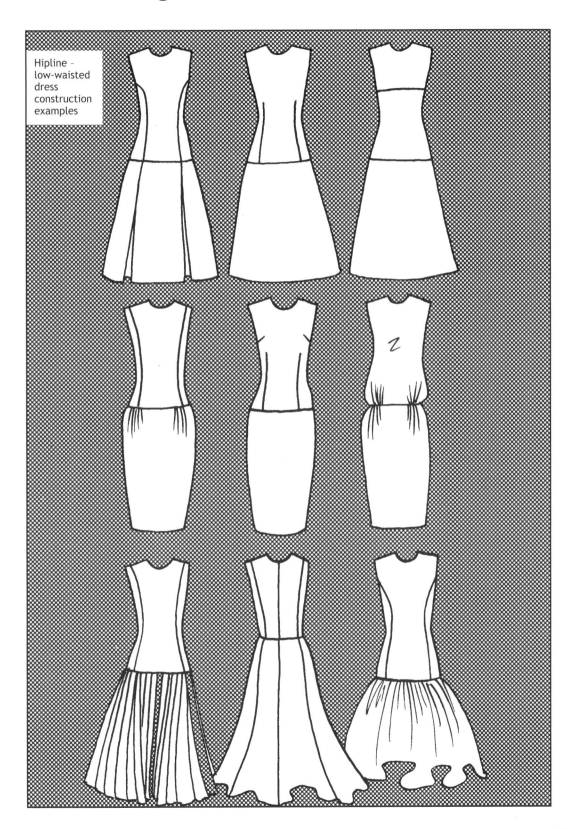

Hipline –
low-waisted
dress
construction
examples

Design Process – Construction – Dresses

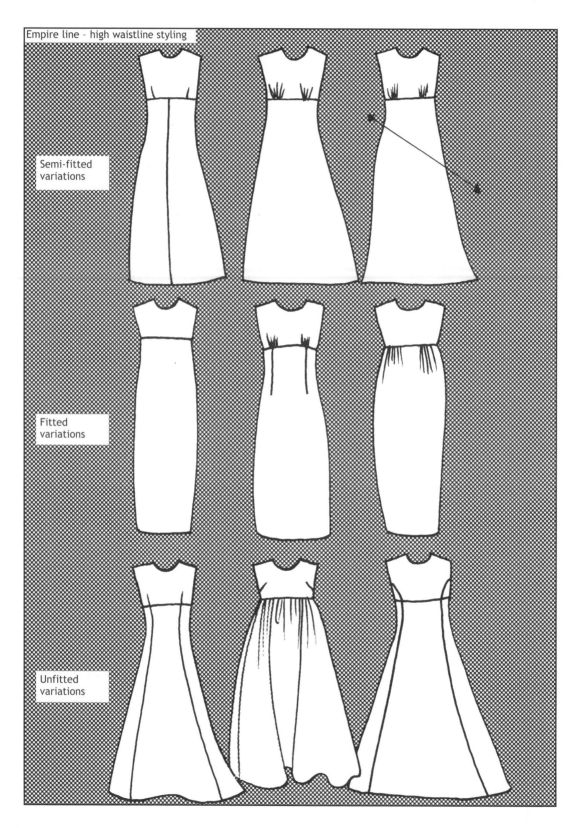

Empire line – high waistline styling

Semi-fitted variations

Fitted variations

Unfitted variations

Design Process – Construction – Basic Sleeves

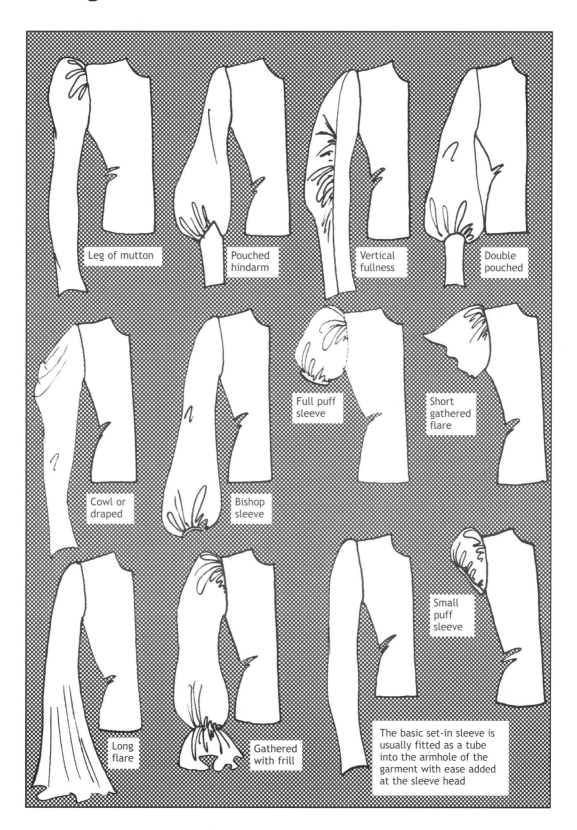

Leg of mutton

Pouched hindarm

Vertical fullness

Double pouched

Cowl or draped

Bishop sleeve

Full puff sleeve

Short gathered flare

Long flare

Gathered with frill

Small puff sleeve

The basic set-in sleeve is usually fitted as a tube into the armhole of the garment with ease added at the sleeve head

Design Process – Construction – Basic Sleeves

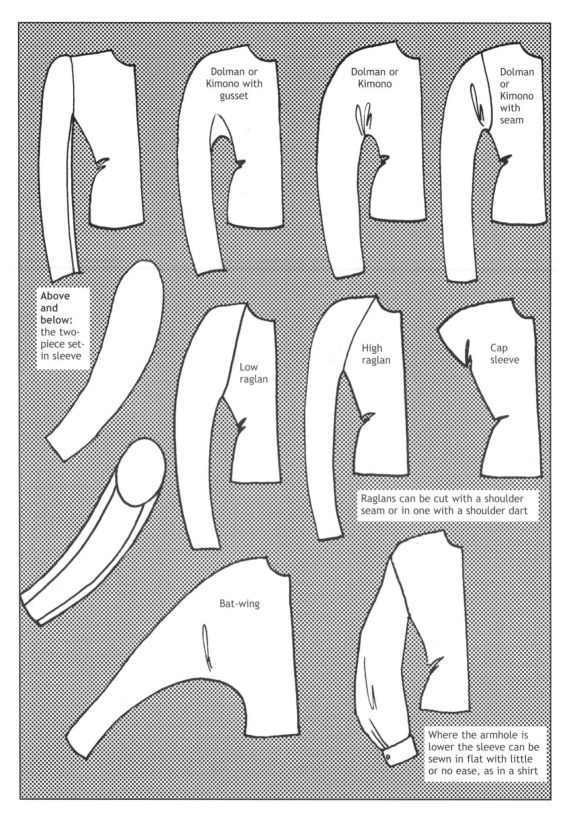

Dolman or Kimono with gusset

Dolman or Kimono

Dolman or Kimono with seam

Above and below: the two-piece set-in sleeve

Low raglan

High raglan

Cap sleeve

Raglans can be cut with a shoulder seam or in one with a shoulder dart

Bat-wing

Where the armhole is lower the sleeve can be sewn in flat with little or no ease, as in a shirt

Design Process – Construction – Basic Trousers

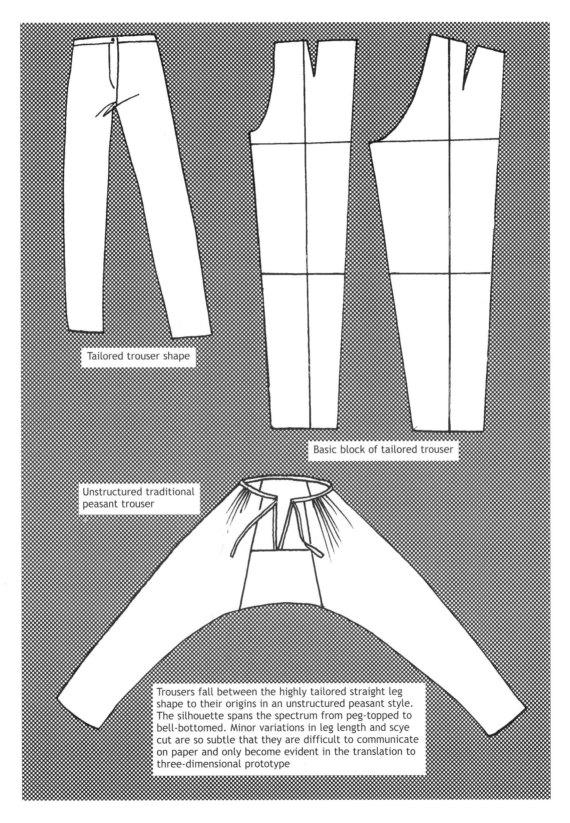

Tailored trouser shape

Basic block of tailored trouser

Unstructured traditional peasant trouser

Trousers fall between the highly tailored straight leg shape to their origins in an unstructured peasant style. The silhouette spans the spectrum from peg-topped to bell-bottomed. Minor variations in leg length and scye cut are so subtle that they are difficult to communicate on paper and only become evident in the translation to three-dimensional prototype

Design Process – Construction – Basic Trousers

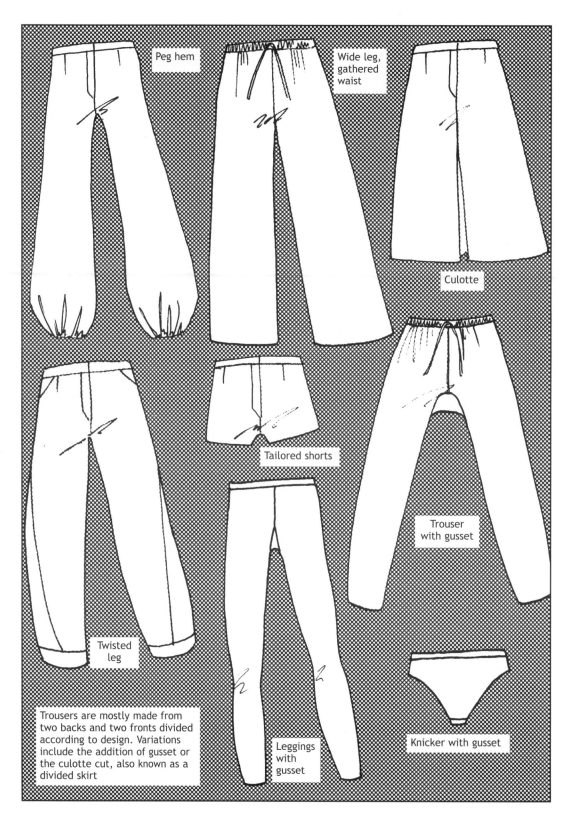

Peg hem

Wide leg, gathered waist

Culotte

Tailored shorts

Twisted leg

Trouser with gusset

Leggings with gusset

Knicker with gusset

Trousers are mostly made from two backs and two fronts divided according to design. Variations include the addition of gusset or the culotte cut, also known as a divided skirt

Design Process – Construction – Basic Trousers

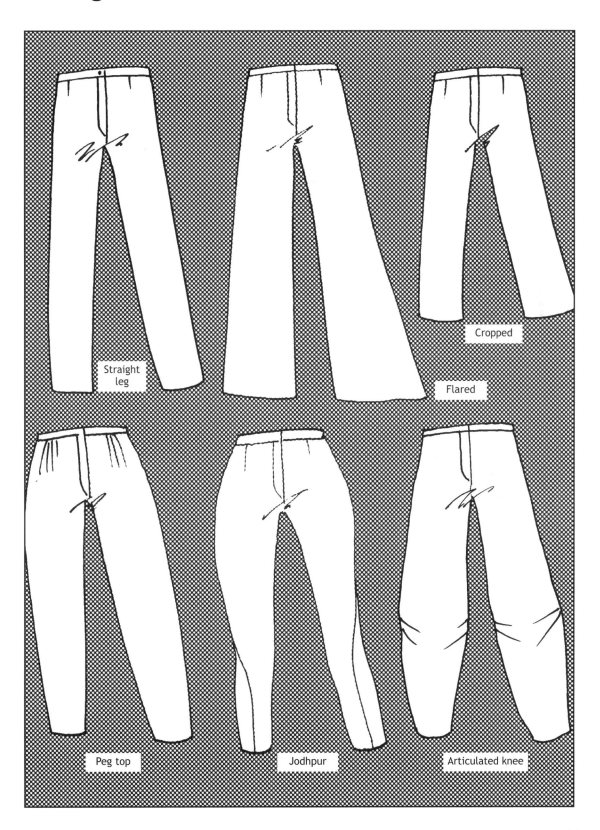

Straight leg

Cropped

Flared

Peg top

Jodhpur

Articulated knee

Design Process – Construction – Basic Collars

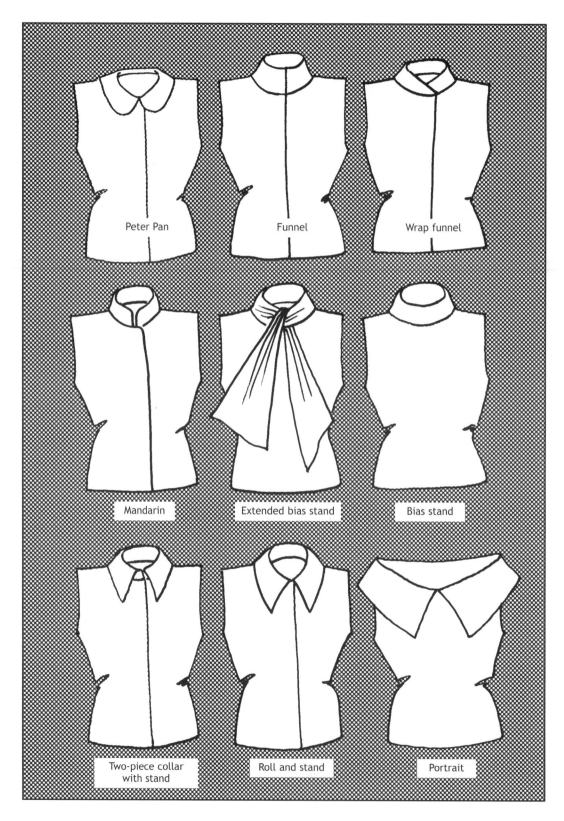

Peter Pan

Funnel

Wrap funnel

Mandarin

Extended bias stand

Bias stand

Two-piece collar with stand

Roll and stand

Portrait

Design Process – Construction – Basic Collars

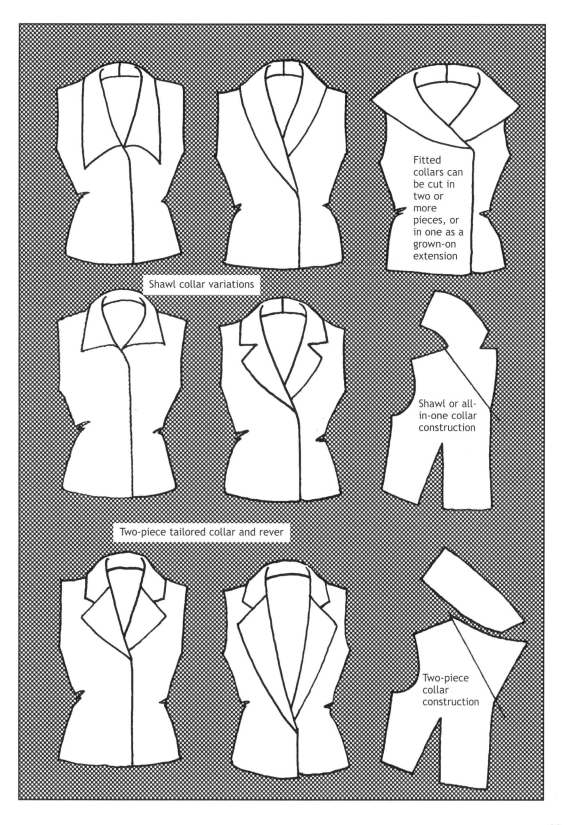

Fitted collars can be cut in two or more pieces, or in one as a grown-on extension

Shawl collar variations

Shawl or all-in-one collar construction

Two-piece tailored collar and rever

Two-piece collar construction

Design Process – Prototypes

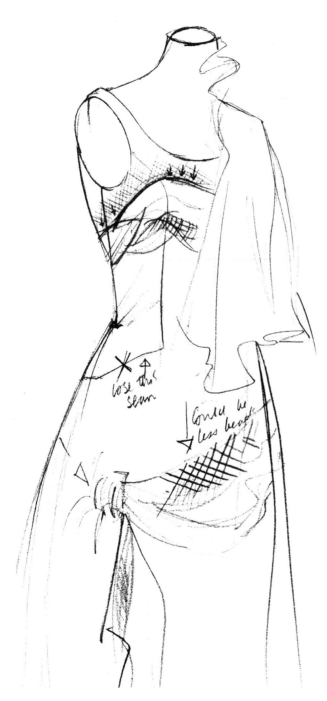

In the design process the translation of a two-dimensional drawn idea into a three-dimensional prototype is the essential element in the realisation of a successful garment design.

At different points in the history of fashion, the closeness of fit to the body shape becomes more or less significant according to the whim of the time. Most designs fit the body closely at some point; this may be the bodice, hips, sleeves, or the whole body shape. It is important, therefore, in order to create a three-dimensional garment, to understand how fabric works with the body, and in particular to know how it can be cut to hang well and enhance the human form. These skills are learned over a number of years, with experience of different fabric capabilities, knowledge of flat pattern cutting, modelling on the stand and an understanding of the human body.

This translation stage is one of experimentation and evaluation. A prototype of the design is made and fitted on a mannequin or model; traditionally calico or muslin is used. However, in mass production this stage is usually carried out in the intended fabric and called a 'first sample'. In some companies there is a dedicated 'toilist' whose sole job is to understand the drawings of the designer and translate these into prototypes. At this stage any design problems can be resolved.

When the toile is on a mannequin or model, designing continues with the manipulation of the fabric to perfect the shape in addition to shaping and positioning of seams, pocket positioning and other details.

Black tape can be pinned to the toile in order to create strong lines from which to assess the proportionate effect of seam lines or trimmings.

New lines and written instructions can be marked on the toile.

Design Process – Prototypes

In order to make a garment fit properly, it is important to have an understanding of the human body. The most important factor in the successful design, balance and fit of a garment is the correct distribution of the waist suppression. This is the method used in order to cut or smooth away the excess fabric at the waist. The principle involved is that a curve is longer than a straight line between two given points. This being so, length must be allowed for and provided to enable the garment to follow the natural curves of the figure. Reducing fabric just at the side seams will result in incorrect fitting as the figure requires the excess amount to be reduced at the side back and front (see diagrams) to allow for the bust curves and the curve of the back.

In order to make a garment fit the figure shape succinctly the following two main methods can be used. Many designs rely upon a mixture of these methods.

FLAT PATTERN CUTTING

This method involves the cutting and seaming of the fabric in order to fit the figure whilst maintaining the correct hang of the fabric. A system of pattern cutting has evolved over time in line with the development of mass production. This method involves the use of cardboard blocks that provide a well-fitting shape, which closely fits the figure but retains the correct balance, waist suppression and fit. The pattern is then made into a first sample or muslin toile and the fit is perfected on a model. Blocks are developed to suit the prevailing fashionable body shape and are purpose-built for the product that the company wishes to produce.

Most pattern cutters adapt the block to the specifications of the designer, as detailed in their drawings and notes, by using a pattern drafting system in order to achieve a balanced and well-fitting approximation of the design. How the pattern cutter decides to interpret the drawing is a matter of skill and intuition, and its successful outcome a mark of the understanding in the relationship between the designer and the pattern cutter.

TOILE MODELLING

Some garments are developed not by blocks but by modelling patterns in toile. The method involves modelling in calico or muslin directly on to the stand or figure.

In the hands of a skilled toilist, modelling patterns become as accurate and simple as drafting on the flat. The most practical method is that of fitting the exact outline of the stand or figure with a muslin shell with care being taken to obtain a perfect fit by the use of panel seams and darts. While this perfect shape is on the stand, the lines of the design are marked in with chalk or pencil and then transferred from the model to a flat pattern. This method is also used for draped and complicated styles.

Design Process – Prototypes

In most garments the lengthwise grain runs from top to bottom of the body in order to allow the weft grain to run around the body utilising its greater elasticity. This creates ease over the shoulders and body making them more comfortable to wear. Lengthwise grain hangs better than crosswise. Fabrics tear more easily lengthwise than crosswise.

Lengthwise grain in fabrics identifies the threads that run parallel to the selvedge (the non-fraying edge) and these are known as the warp; the threads which run from left to right at 90 degrees to the selvedge are called the weft.

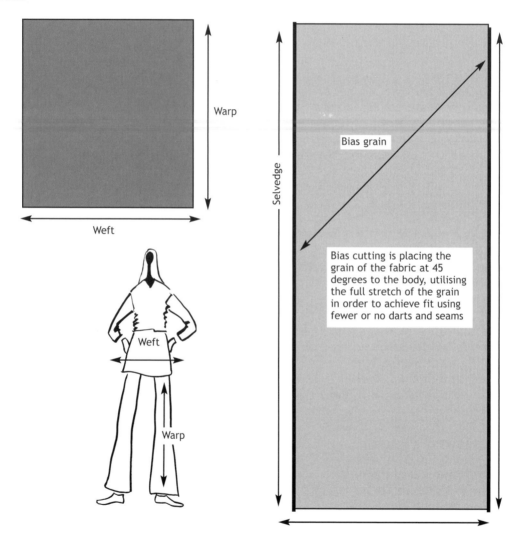

Warp

Weft

Selvedge

Bias grain

Bias cutting is placing the grain of the fabric at 45 degrees to the body, utilising the full stretch of the grain in order to achieve fit using fewer or no darts and seams

Weft

Warp

The term 'off-grain' is used to describe a fabric fault where the warp and weft are not at right angles to each other. Garments that are cut without understanding of the correct use of the grain can have disastrous results, hanging unevenly; trousers can twist around the legs.

Equally designs that fully utilise the fabric's best qualities, and the ease and stretch of the appropriate grains, are generally most successful.

A 'one-way' fabric can only be cut out in one direction because of its properties, such as the print design, nap, pile or weave.

Design Process – Prototypes

UTILISING FABRIC PROPERTIES IN CONSTRUCTION

The quality and handle of the chosen fabric(s) for the intended design is of great importance. Whether this is woven, knitted, patterned or textured they all will have an effect on the type of construction method used.

BIAS CUTTING

This method involves using the bias grain of the fabric in order to utilise the stretch qualities of this grain in fitting to the figure.

From time to time bias cutting becomes fashionable as a method of fitting the figure by moulding a sheath outline to the figure without waist seams, darts or design seams to help. The term bias cutting means cutting the dress on the cross or bias of the fabric.

Bias fabric stretches as follows: if one part of the material is stretched out, the part immediately above it is narrowed in. Normally the bust and hip measurements are cut smaller than the figure to decrease the width of the dress through the waist and so cause sufficient length to be created at the side seams to enable the garment to follow the curves of the figure. If the hip size of the garment is cut smaller than the figure the action of stretching the fabric will result in a flare of the skirt at the hemline. If this were cut on the straight a perfectly straight tube would result.

Bias cutting is used in lingerie design for slips, chemise tops and camisoles where a close-fitting shape is necessary. This can be achieved with no fastenings on a woven fabric. Bias cutting is also important to give vivacity and flexibility to frills, flounces and certain collars.

STRETCH FABRICS

Stretch or knitted fabrics can reduce the need for seams in order to fit neatly on the body. Stretch fabrics have revolutionised garment cutting; there is less need for complicated darts and seaming with the fit relying upon the quality of the fabric employed. When constructing toiles for stretch designs it is important to try to use a fabric with the same amount of stretch and recovery as the intended end-use fabric, as the result will be inaccurate, either being too tight or too loose.

STRUCTURE

Most garments have some form of interlining in order to reinforce part of the garment – the collar and cuffs, for example. Interlinings are used in many ways to give support to delicate or loosely woven fabrics; they exaggerate appearance and create a different handle to the fabric.

Design Process – Prototypes

It is easy to lose sight of your original intentions during the translation stage; try keeping your design drawings close to hand and refer to them to check if your shape looks the same.

Although it may take some time to gain experience in pattern cutting, one of the first principles to learn is the relationship between the shape of the basic cardboard blocks, the dress stand and the body. These three shapes are different.

The block has ease added so that it fits around the body snugly but allows for movement, particularly over the areas that need most movement such as the shoulder blade. The dress stand is a solid representation of the standard size body shape; it does not have the subtleties of the human body. These stands can be purchased in any size and shape and are extremely sophisticated. However, prototypes need to be seen in movement on a model to assess the final design.

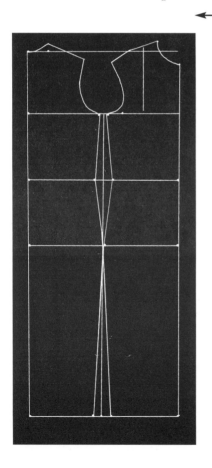 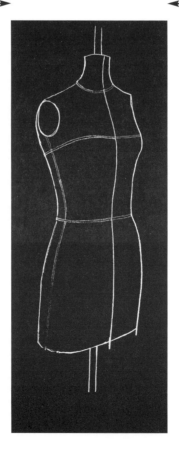 

Basic block draft of dress with shoulder and waist darts.

A toile is either cut from the initial pattern or modelled directly on to the stand in order to assess the correct balance and fit. At this stage the designer has to ensure that the original intention of the drawn design is fully realised.

Design Process – Prototypes

Dress block draft of basic dress with bust dart and waist shaping.

Dress block draft with shoulder dart.

Creating a basic dress toile with bust dart and waist shaping. The front and backs were modelled first and then a sleeve added.

Design Process – Embellishment

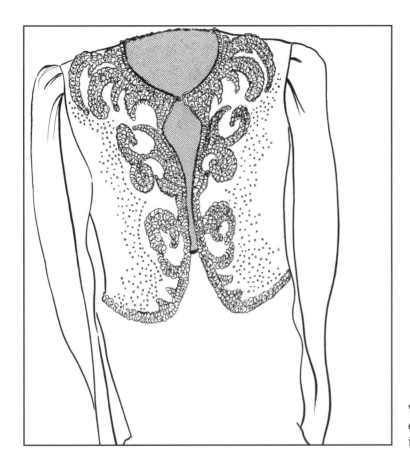

Vintage 1930s black crêpe evening bolero jacket with ivory sequins and beading.

FINISH AND DETAIL

Finish and detail form the decorative part of design; there are many different embellishment processes and design details that drift in and out of popularity. For the purposes of this book, detail and embellishment have been discussed as separate processes; however, they are in practice often combined. There are many different processes involved in the treatment of fabrics both for mass production, completed by outside process specialists, and by hand by skilled craftspeople.

Garments are usually decorated in one of the following ways:

- Fabrics that are patterned, textured or processed before cutting.
  Example: Sequins bought on the roll, any printed fabric.
- Garment pieces that are cut and then patterned, textured or processed before sewing.
  Example: Machine embroidery, screen-printed motifs, pleating.
- The finished garment is patterned, textured or processed.
  Example: Stone washing, dyeing.

Once you have decided on the colour, fabrication, and have created the shape and form of your design, it is time to consider the detail. This stage is extremely important, for the finish of a garment is often what makes the difference between a designer-level garment and one of a lower market level, especially on simple garments. Detail covers everything from frills, flounces, flying panels, pockets, collars, cuffs and fastenings to binding, lining, piping and the size, colour and gauge of the actual stitching.

Design Process – Embellishment

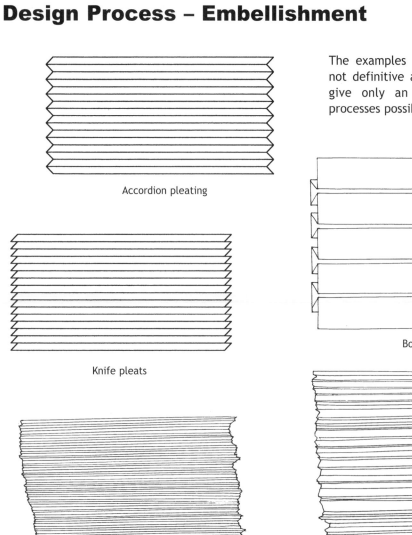

Accordion pleating

The examples illustrated here are not definitive and are intended to give only an indication of the processes possible.

Box pleats

Knife pleats

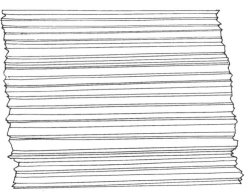

Crystal pleating

Mushroom pleating

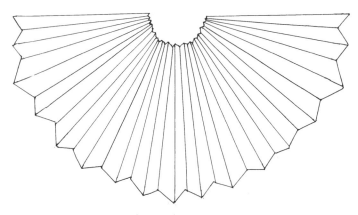

Sunray pleating

Tree bark pleating

Design Process – Embellishment

Picot edge

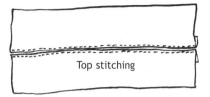
Top stitching

Braids and ribbons

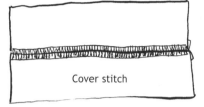
Cover stitch

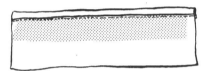
Bias binding

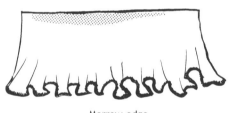
Merrow edge

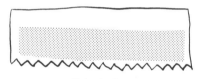
Pinked edge

Fringing

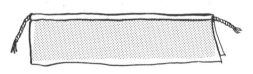
Piping

Raw edge

Scalloped edging

Design Process – Embellishment

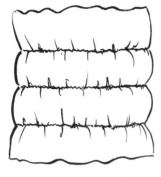

Wide quilting

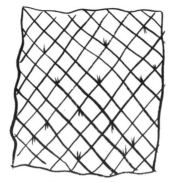

Diamond quilting

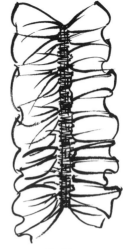

Ruching

Frills

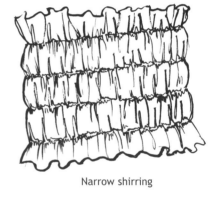

Narrow shirring

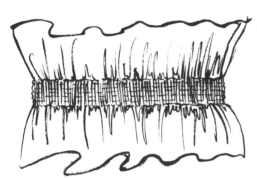

Wide shirring

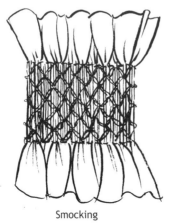

Smocking

Pin-tucks

104

Design Process – Embellishment

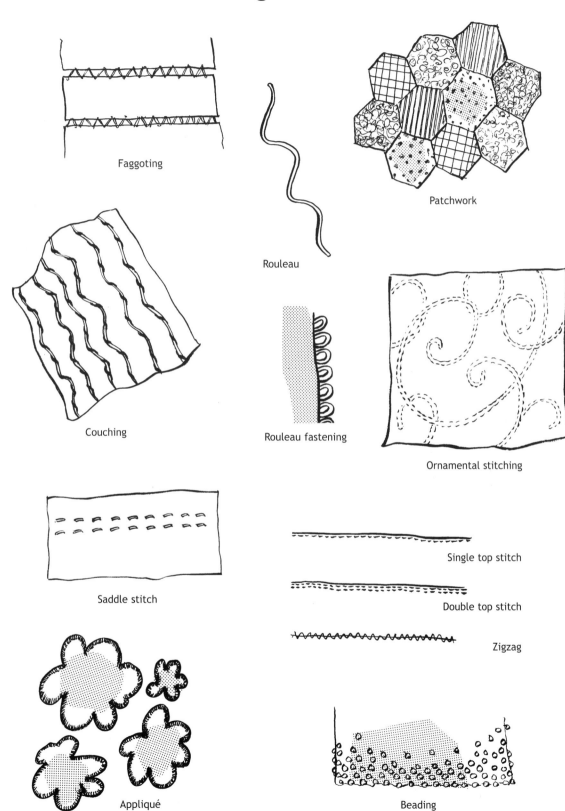

Faggoting

Rouleau

Patchwork

Couching

Rouleau fastening

Ornamental stitching

Saddle stitch

Single top stitch

Double top stitch

Zigzag

Appliqué

Beading

Design Process – Embellishment

Working drawings from an urban utility range illustrating detail and decoration.
Examples courtesy of IN.D.EX, London

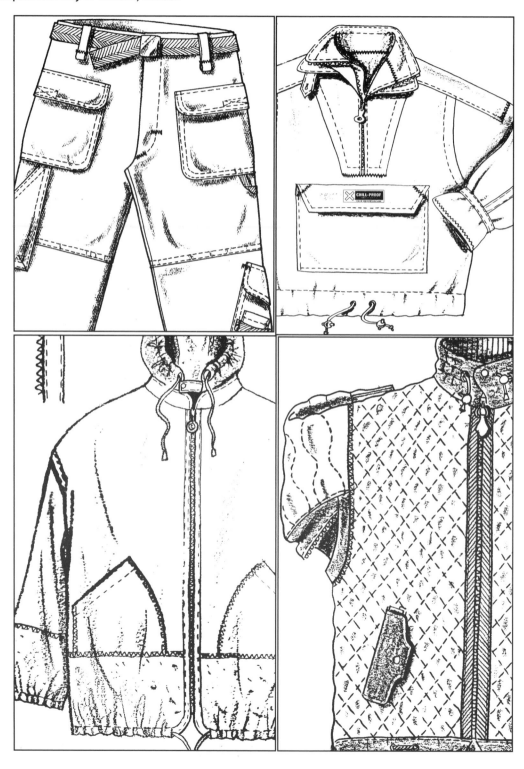

Design Process – Embellishment

The combining of pattern, texture and specialist techniques are the tools for creating strong visual impact. A useful design exercise is to design only in colour, pattern or texture or a combination of these working directly in colour not pencil.

Sometimes the design detail or process can be the main inspiration, for example using oversized or unusual zips, complicated or multiple pockets.

Examples drawn from the Autumn/Winter collections of 2000/2001

Design Process – Embellishment

In this example, derived from a designer collection, the construction/cut is the key. A quirky combination of asymmetry and checked patterning emphasises the cut of the garments.

Examples drawn from the Autumn/Winter collections of 2000/2001

Design Process – Embellishment

In this example, derived from a designer collection, the contrast between dark and light is most apparent, also the use of waisted and high-waisted cuts. The looks are casual with a small amount of tailoring.

Examples drawn from the Autumn/Winter collections of 2000/2001

Design Process – Embellishment

These examples of designer collections show silhouette and a combination of prints and patterns. The waistlines are dropped to the hip and the tops follow the natural body shape. The silhouette is a gentle A-line.

Examples drawn from the Autumn/Winter collections of 2000/2001

Design for Specialist Markets

Most designers eventually become specialists in a particular field. This may be menswear, womenswear, active or non-active sportswear, childrenswear, accessories, footwear, cocktail and eveningwear, bridal, maternity, plus sizes, lingerie or a host of other niche markets. Each specialism has its own trade shows, exhibitions and publications.

Designing for an individual product makes the process of design highly specialised. The designer has to have an in-depth knowledge of the construction and performance of the product and have a complete understanding of the materials and manufacturing processes employed in their production.

Example courtesy of Susie Wells

Example courtesy of Milou Ket Styling and Design

Example courtesy of IN.D.EX, London

111

Design for Specialist Markets

These lingerie designs illustrate the complexity of design required for this product. There can be over 30 different components in a bra; each has to be sourced and put together to create not only an aesthetically pleasing product but one that fits well and is comfortable to wear. Technological developments in fabrics and construction methods now make this type of design more science based.

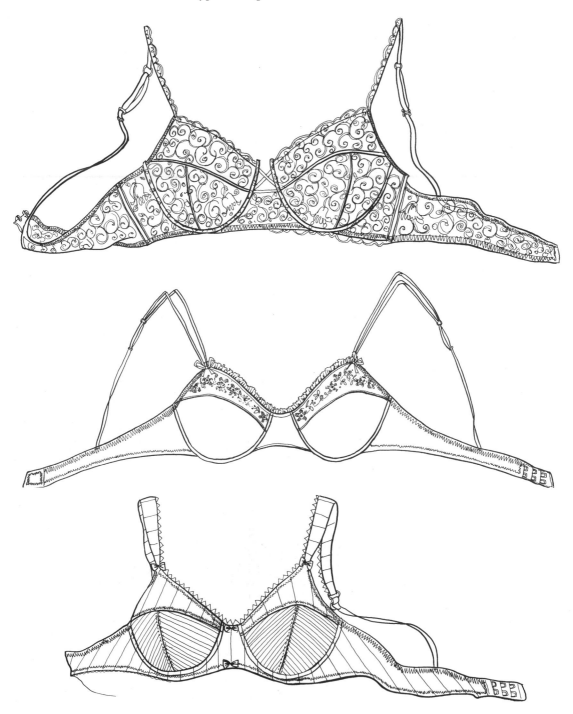

Designing Ranges and Collections

DESIGNING RANGES AND COLLECTIONS

There are commercial considerations for the professional designer to take into account when putting together a collection, for example the target market and the lifestyle of the customer. How will forthcoming fashion trends fit with the brand or design philosophy of the company? Other factors include seasonal or climatic considerations of the intended domestic or export market, and the cost, economy and ease of manufacture.

RANGE PLANNING

Range planning involves the devising of the ratio of garments to be designed in any given collection. For example a basic range may consist of four skirts, three trousers, six tops, two jackets and two dresses in three colourways. Every collection needs to have a breakdown of units so that the customer can have the right choice and be able to put together a combination of outfits. If more volume sales come from tops or suits then it makes sense to provide more of these in the collection.

The aesthetic considerations of designing a collection are subjective, a matter for the viewer and wearer's individual taste. However, there are some general principles that can be analysed. Most collections have an underlying theme even if it is one of chaos! This can be a recognisable theme or storyline, for instance a romantic or nautical look, or it could be a more abstract theme based on a line, or geometric shape, for example. Many designers have a personal style or handwriting that is constant, with minor changes in line with long-term trends.

The intended destination of the collection has a large impact on the colour and weight of fabrics selected. Compare these assessments of best sellers from the fashion capitals of the world during winter 2000; although there are similarities, there are trends specific to the individual cities.

PARIS

Shapes – wide-shouldered chic suits, below-knee skirts and trousers with turn-ups, blouses and vintage dresses, flounced skirts.
Colour – brown, red, beige and caramel; also pink, yellow and orange.
Print – Art Deco and geometric.
Fabric – fake fur and leather, luxurious and rustic wools, men's suitings.
Influences – Lauren Bacall, Audrey Hepburn.

TOKYO

Shapes – retro seventies-style coats, slim skirts and blazers, three-quarter sleeves, little black dresses, blouses, twin sets.
Colour – camel, beige brown, olive, sage and khaki, marigold, mandarin, grape, cobalt blue, pink and black.
Fabric – tweed, check, tartan, cashmere corduroy, velvet, denim, herringbone, hand knits.
Influences – the 'jet set', romanticism, retro styling.

LONDON

Shapes – wide shoulder lines, batwings, A-line or pencil skirts, knee length, jackets straight and cropped, suits, culottes.
Colour – monotone, gold, bronze, sand, chocolate, aubergine, magenta, green.
Print – checks and stripes, geometric, large 1950s florals.
Fabric – metallic and glitter effects, sequins, chiffon and jersey, leathers and suede.
Influences – Dynasty, early Madonna, Grace Jones.

Designing Ranges and Collections

Thematic collection based on buccaneers. Impact relies on the use of nautical and utilitarian fabrics, styling and accessories.

Examples taken from Paris catwalk collections for Spring/Summer 2000

Designing Ranges and Collections

This part of a collection is based on the decorative use of large-scale arcs and the making of a strong impact with contrasting geometric divisions. The floral print is also given a circular treatment.

Examples taken from Paris catwalk collections for Spring/Summer 2000

Designing Ranges and Collections

Part of a simple collection whose impact relies upon subtle use of colour, texture, fabric and finish.

Examples taken from Paris catwalk collections for Spring/Summer 2000

Designing Ranges and Collections

Decision Making

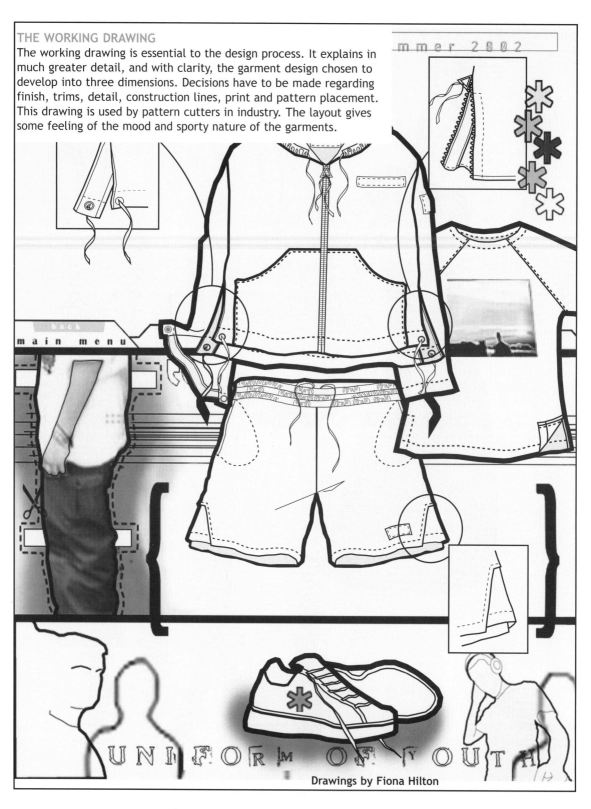

THE WORKING DRAWING

The working drawing is essential to the design process. It explains in much greater detail, and with clarity, the garment design chosen to develop into three dimensions. Decisions have to be made regarding finish, trims, detail, construction lines, print and pattern placement. This drawing is used by pattern cutters in industry. The layout gives some feeling of the mood and sporty nature of the garments.

Drawings by Fiona Hilton

Decision Making

THE RANGE PLAN

In addition to decisions about each individual garment, the balance of the range as a whole needs to be considered. Is there the right amount of texture, pattern, print or simply interest? Does the colour balance well? Does the range offer enough impact?

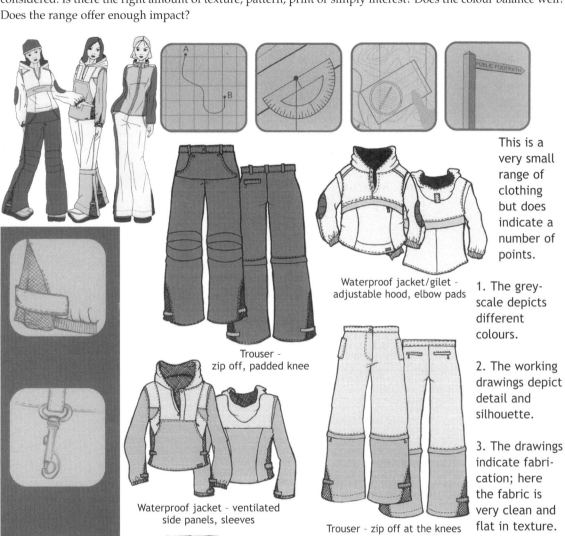

Waterproof jacket/gilet –
adjustable hood, elbow pads

Trouser –
zip off, padded knee

Waterproof jacket – ventilated
side panels, sleeves

Trouser – zip off at the knees

Trouser with side panels

Jacket – zip-away hood

Drawings by
Carolyn Berry

This is a very small range of clothing but does indicate a number of points.

1. The grey-scale depicts different colours.

2. The working drawings depict detail and silhouette.

3. The drawings indicate fabri-cation; here the fabric is very clean and flat in texture.

4. The figure drawings are helpful in showing the proportion of the garments in comparison to each other, how they should be worn, the attitude and target market.

Design Using the Computer

This section could be called 'computer-aided design' (CAD); it does not use 'fashion industry standard' software packages, but software used by the 'new media' and graphic design industries to realise ideas. This software is creeping into all sorts of work and here Adobe Illustrator is used to illustrate a working or technical drawing. The primary function of a working drawing is that it clearly communicates the designer's intentions regarding construction, fabrication, detail, trim, fastenings and finish.

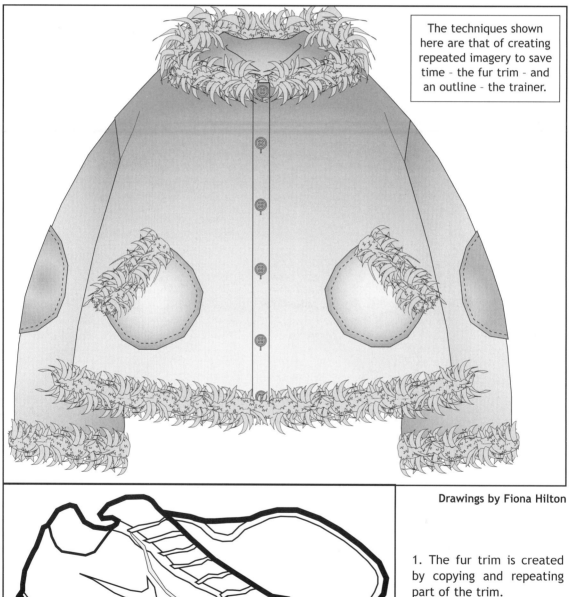

> The techniques shown here are that of creating repeated imagery to save time – the fur trim – and an outline – the trainer.

Drawings by Fiona Hilton

1. The fur trim is created by copying and repeating part of the trim.
2. The outline is created by selecting a line thickness, using the 'pen' tool in Adobe Illustrator, and using layers to create the details.

Design Using the Computer

DIGITAL WORKING DRAWINGS

Sophisticated working drawings can be produced using Adobe Illustrator. It is possible to import photographic style images and impose them upon T-shirts for a realistic representation of a design. It is also possible to introduce shading and texture to differentiate between areas so that the drawing becomes clearer and has a three-dimensional feel. The detail boxes enlarge selected areas, clarifying specific trims and finishes

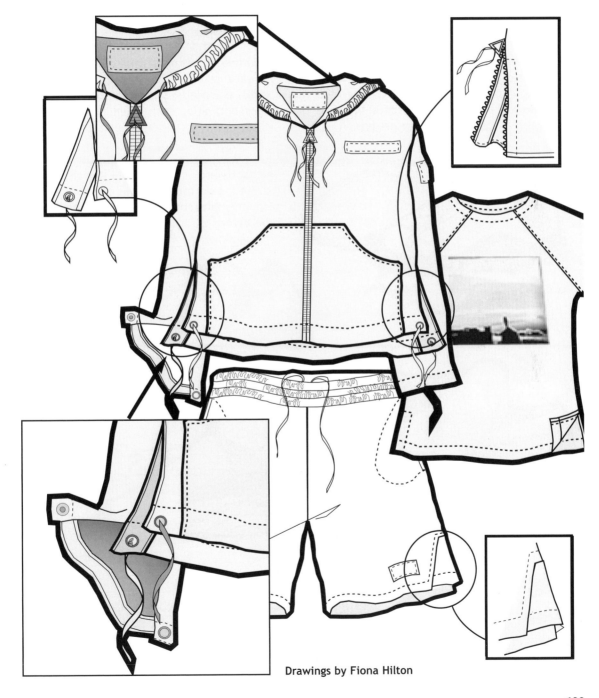

Drawings by Fiona Hilton

Design Using the Computer

Computer software may also be used to repeat a shape, outline or silhouette so that a variety of treatments may be applied. Once the user has gained experience and skill this can save a lot of time. The results are often sophisticated due to the versatility of the medium – adding shading, repetitive detail and decoration. Colour can be altered simply by selecting and clicking – colour palettes for a whole season can be displayed and compared on screen. Designing ranges and working with colour combinations becomes simpler. The *Pantone Colour Specifier System* can help to inform about accurate colour when printing from the computer if the colour code numbers are used. Print-outs may be used for presentations of ranges to buyers and merchandisers, and as aids to the designer, the pattern cutter, the retailer and the visual merchandiser.

These women's training shoes were designed by using an outline of a training shoe. The drawing was repeated and five different approaches to the design were taken – the lace-up, the boot-like elasticated gusset, the elasticated mule effect, the shoe-like elasticated gusset and the 'sling-back' shoe. There are strong relationships between the designs but, also, each could be the start of propagating a whole set of other designs.

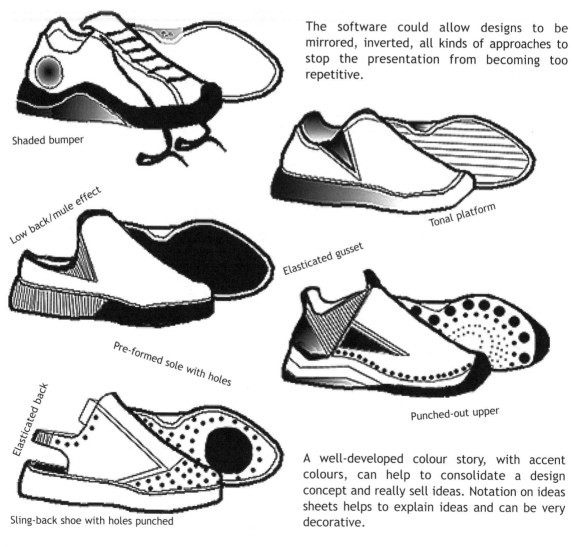

Shaded bumper

The software could allow designs to be mirrored, inverted, all kinds of approaches to stop the presentation from becoming too repetitive.

Low back/mule effect

Tonal platform

Elasticated gusset

Pre-formed sole with holes

Punched-out upper

Elasticated back

Sling-back shoe with holes punched

A well-developed colour story, with accent colours, can help to consolidate a design concept and really sell ideas. Notation on ideas sheets helps to explain ideas and can be very decorative.

Design Using the Computer

Desktop publishing software is very useful when working with graphics and visuals. It is possible to create sophisticated imagery with layers of information. Digital cameras have improved dramatically in quality over the years and can be useful tools for inputting 'first generation' images into the computer. Photographs can be directly downloaded on to the hard drive and then manipulated in a piece of image editing software such as Adobe PhotoShop.

This picture was taken with a digital camera and then placed into the computer.

The image was 'inverted', that is, the colours were switched to their opposites in the spectrum. This provides a more unusual image to that expected and makes the colour much more vivid.

The photographic image can then be imported into software such as QuarkXPress and text may be placed where required.

The image was increased in size to give the appearance of a more abstract visual. The colours were used as a basis for the 'Corporate Identity'. See the 'Case Study' (p. 153) for more development ideas.

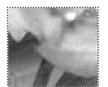
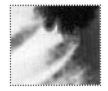

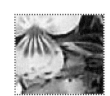

Design Using the Computer

The computer has been used by the fashion industry for many years in the generation of print ideas. It is possible to repeat, rotate, invert, mirror and apply all kinds of effects to printed textile ideas. Print repeats can be achieved simply and cheaply depending upon the required market level.

A single photographic image is rotated and placed over a larger photographic image in the background. The colour is true to the plant.

This is a very simplistic print which was generated from a hand-rendered paper 'monoprint'. The monoprint provides rough 'visual' texture in contrast to the smoothness of the photographic image. (See Case Study – Print Development.)

The print motif was inverted to provide blocks of contrast. The two were then combined to make the print. This is a one-way print.

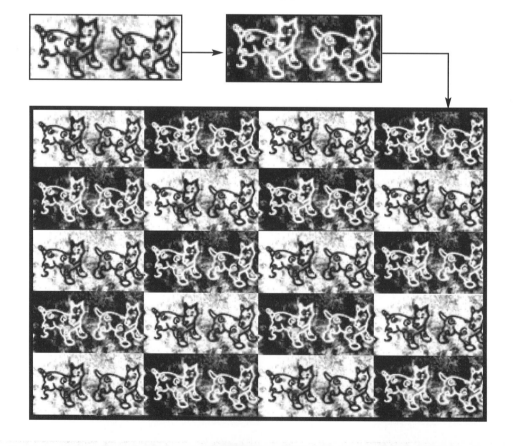

Design Using the Computer

COMPUTER-AIDED DESIGN SOFTWARE

The computer can be a helpful aid when producing design development sheets showing a range or collection. The whole collection may be repeated with emphasis on a different printed textile each time. Such software as Tex Design and Primavision Design are traditional pieces of computer-aided design (CAD) software used in the fashion industry.

The print is loaded and repeated using the 'pattern stamp tool' in Adobe PhotoShop. The print can be 'drawn on' where required. The scale of the print may be varied.

knitted pants

beaded bag

striped hat

frilly hat

all-in-one with frill

donkey hat

dress with donkey print inverted

all-in-one doggy stripe print

all-in-one with feet - print

bodysuit with donkey print

baseball boot with rubber platform

doggy print shoe

pants with knee pads

printed vest

frilly all-in-one

doggy printed pants

printed hat

donkey print pyjamas

piggy hat

dress with satin ribbon

kitty purse

pleated frill hat

quartered all-in-one with doggy print

doggy print baseball boot

printed leggings with ribbing

piggy bodysuit

bodysuit with puffed sleeves

Design Using the Computer

DESIGNING WITH INTERACTIVE MEDIA

Ideas have to be communicated to the client. It is possible to create presentations by 'authoring' interactive projects using such tools as Macromedia Director. Digital video is also a very useful medium where footage may be shot using a digital video camera recorder. The visuals may be downloaded on to a computer's hard drive and edited in video editing software such as Adobe Premiere. A variety of effects may be applied to highlight certain points using such software as Adobe After Effects.

When using different media it is useful to produce a 'storyboard' highlighting key actions and sound effects. These may be exciting visuals in their own right and act as a prompt when working in a team. It is also helpful to produce a 'flowchart' which indicates a hierarchy of computer screens, starting with the menu page/contents followed by the actual content.

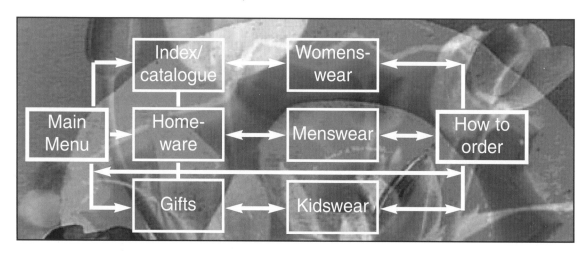

Promotion/Graphics

PROMOTING THE RANGE

The identity of the range is continued into promotional activities. Normally this is a graphics job, but a blurring of design disciplines allows fashion and graphics to cross over. Fashion designers can apply their skills and knowledge to a new area and market their own concepts. T-shirts have been designed for years with prints and logos emblazoned on the front. Branding over recent years has become central to promoting and marketing fashion goods.

The branding process requires the range to have a 'name'. Producing a name requires some thought regarding the personal philosophy of the range and how this can be interpreted into an evocative word or words.

Interesting uses of the language can produce visual effects, such as, iMac (Internet ready Macintosh computer), One2One (cell phone company), FCUK (French Connection United Kingdom), brand.new (taking advantage of the interest in all things Internet by using the dot).

You should begin by researching contemporary graphics.

Brainstorm a name:

1. Use a thesaurus.
2. Try to translate an ordinary word into a different language!

Once a name has been chosen it has to be 'dressed up' to reflect whatever the range is trying to communicate. This involves the use of fonts, scale, colour and perhaps a logo.

Try enlarging, reducing and modifying the identity and apply it to swing tickets and hanger labels, flyers, packaging, advertising and even transport livery.

'VISUAL LANGUAGE is the "look and feel" of an item of design – created by such elements as colour, proportion, letterform, shape, texture ... It conveys emotional messages to its audiences and they "feel" something about the client, service or product.'
From *Visual Language: the Hidden Meaning of Communication*, Peter Bonnici, RotoVision, 1998

'WEAR ME: fashion+graphics interaction is about the symbiotic relationship between the graphic designer and fashion designer. The two are inextricably linked, not only in the conventional creative/client partnership, but because each discipline possesses its own unique visual history and vocabulary.

Signs and symbols are the stock in trade of both worlds. Fashion designers and graphic designers are adept at reading, interpreting and appropriating visual codes. That they stray into each other's territory is proof of just how rich these sources of mutual sampling can be.'
From *WEAR ME: fashion+graphics interaction*, edited by Liz Farrelly, Booth Clibborn Editions, 1995

'The idea of the brand is central to contemporary society. Businesses, personalities, political parties and even nations "re-brand" themselves in order to influence public opinion ... Today's brands promote themselves as more than just a logo, a slogan or a distinctive package, they promise to deliver a host of emotional benefits too.'
brand.new, edited by Jane Pavitt, V&A Publications, 2000

Promotion/Styling

THE PHOTOGRAPHIC SHOOT

The photographic shoot provides another opportunity to promote the range by styling as the designer intended, or to fit a specific theme or 'story' that a magazine may be promoting. There are a variety of questions to ask:

What are you trying to achieve? What is the ultimate purpose of the styling and photographs? Is it/are they visually eye-catching? Are you conveying the correct message according to your market and design research? Is it your intention to attract, shock, inform or amuse? Have you given the photographer enough time to sort out any special needs, that is, special films or lenses, gels, or filters?

WORKING ON IDEAS

It helps to stay focused – variations on a theme work much better than moving, ad hoc, from one idea to another. It is also less time-consuming and time can be very expensive in the studio. The stylist works with the photographer and will direct the shoot. The photographer will take care of all of the technical requirements.

THE MOOD

Plan carefully how you want the photographs to look! Is your background wide enough for long shots, or high enough for perspective shots from below? Does the mood match the market level, brand, personality, identity?

BACKDROPS AND PROPS

The shoot could take place in the studio or on location.

Backdrops/props are important; you need to consider the colour and scale of the backdrop or provide your own draped fabrics, painted backdrops or textural surfaces.

What are the logistics of moving the shoot to a location?

POSES/CAMERA ANGLES

A good selection of pose ideas or camera angles should be available at the shoot. Four or five different poses will not be enough!

LIGHTING

Use magazines and books for ideas on lighting. Show these to the photographer at the planning stage and again at the time of the shoot.

THE MODEL

Good models are crucial to a successful shoot. You could take test polaroids of models to see if they are photogenic, or if they are professional, look carefully at their portfolio.

HAIR/MAKE-UP

The 'look' is very important in any styling shoot. Consider the model from all angles, look at their silhouette to check for any potential problems, for example creases and folds, and hair sticking out in the wrong places.

The Portfolio

The portfolio gives you the opportunity to show your versatility. Show work that is visually stimulating and contributes to your breadth of experience. Add work relevant to your current job interview and do your research about the company.

Employers may be looking for specialism in a particular area rather than a general approach.

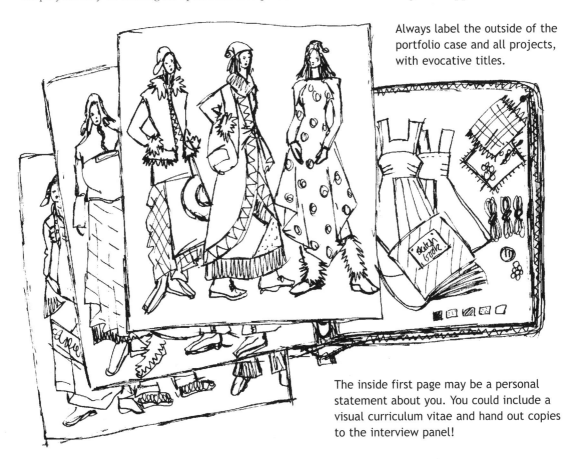

Always label the outside of the portfolio case and all projects, with evocative titles.

The inside first page may be a personal statement about you. You could include a visual curriculum vitae and hand out copies to the interview panel!

Logically organise your work so that similar projects are together and that the sequence is: research material (be it sketchbook or drawn sheets) followed by your best design development sheets, then the final chosen range or collection or product.

You may find that sometimes media such as floppy and zip disks may be included in your portfolio. Package these items in the same way as you would sketchbooks and put covers on them – provide pockets to support them. Sketchbooks can be strung into the ring binder at the appropriate places. Do put covers on them reflecting the project that they belong to.

Arrange your work so that each project is either portrait or landscape – do not mix formats within a project. Create spreads of work that give impact!

Plastic sleeves can be cleaned with lighter fluid; occasionally inks are absorbed into the plastic and stain the surface and also photocopy toner sticks to the sleeves over time.

If you do work on digital media take a laptop computer with you to display your work – do not rely on the panel to provide equipment unless previously arranged.

Fashion Careers – Press Assistant

CAREER OPPORTUNITIES IN THE FASHION INDUSTRY

Graduating students, students who take work placements and personnel already working in the industry, are often unaware of the career potential in the fashion industry. This chapter attempts to explain some of the initial career possibilities and the variety available when using the design skills outlined in this book.

THE PRESS ASSISTANT

The general duties of an in-house press assistant, within a design company, are that of sending out and checking in-press samples, faxing contacts, inputting stock levels on to the computerised stock allocation programme, printing out and picking lists for distribution purposes, printing out invoices and proformas and the ubiquitous photocopying, postal duties, general errands and making the tea!

The press may request samples for photographic shoots; their needs have to be established, i.e. the nature of the shoot, purpose, colour story and theme. The press assistant selects samples from the sample store. Once the items are chosen a press sample form has to be completed and the articles are despatched.

The assistant may help create the press pack which is used for promotional purposes – trade shows and media mail-outs. Depending upon the size of the company, the assistant may help with overall layout of the press pack, sourcing graphics, printing and finishing.
A press pack wallet is required to hold leaves of paper, a business card and represent the image of the company in an aesthetically pleasing and relevant way.

PRESS ASSISTANT

Some of the key elements to being a successful in-house press assistant are:

• Create interest and inform.

• Provide an overview of that season's range by highlighting key silhouettes, the colour palette, fabrics and key pieces.

• Provide photographs in slide format (high-quality reproduction from a slide) of the key items for reproduction into print.

The press assistant organises promotional parties – the venue, lighting, sound, the printing of invitations and the organisation of refreshments.
Overdue clothing samples are chased up by assertive telephone calls and faxes. Magazines and newspapers are acquired with the relevant press clippings and tributes to the company.

Fashion Careers – Public Relations

PUBLIC RELATIONS ASSISTANT

Companies that sell goods or services to the public need to generate interest in their product. This can be anything from a small advert in a local paper to a commercial on national television. This really depends on the company, what it sells, and who it wants to sell to. This interest is generated by the public relations or PR company.

Large businesses may have in-house PR (public relations) who deal permanently and exclusively with the company's publicity requirements. Some large fashion houses like Prada and Versace do this; other companies use independent PR companies to handle their publicity and are referred to as clients.

Usually each client is represented in the PR company showroom by a display of their products available for the press to view. The PR company will develop individual press coverage for each client and produce publicity and promotional campaigns that reflect the current requirements of the client and also anticipate the future needs of the markets at home and abroad.

The PR company needs to know what image the client wants to portray and the market it wants to attract. The media are used to broadcast and generate interest in the product both nationally and internationally by means of events such as fashion shows, press days viewing new products, and parties.

During London Fashion Week account holders will organise the showing of collections. The PR company needs experience in show production – from commissioning the show team, that is show producer, hair and make-up, stylist, house video to venue search, guest list, invitation production and distribution, and the seating plan. The PR company would also work with other PR companies to ensure all foreign press are invited to such events.

Celebrities may be invited to wear clients' clothes and press cuttings should be collected from newspapers and magazines to show how often the client was featured. The account handler must ensure that the clients' products appear in the relevant media.

Part of the 'promotions' exercise is the 'magazine styling shoot'. Stylists contact the PR company to borrow clothing from clients' collections.

Once the stylist has chosen the required products they are booked out on computer, packed into bags and then sent by bike directly to the shoot or to the magazine.

Thousands of pounds worth of merchandise have to be carefully logged in and out. Clothes that are damaged or not returned must be chased by the PR office.

As the seasons change so the products change; the showroom must look immaculate – clothes may need to be pressed.

PUBLIC RELATIONS AND THE CLIENT

Fashion Careers – Assistant Buyer

GENERAL DUTIES OF THE ASSISTANT BUYER

General duties of the Assistant Buyer for a high street fashion retailer could be such tasks as meeting and greeting clients, chasing production, processing orders, maintaining office stock, collating and sending samples to the press, general errands and telephone enquiries.

The buyer decides which styles are finally sold in the shop. They discuss quality and prices through negotiation with the supplier. A legal order is compiled with four different coded copies:

- The *white* copy is the top copy and is sent to the supplier listing the legalities, terms and conditions of the contract.
- The *yellow* copy is filed by the allocator for reference and pre-allocations.
- The *green* copy is filed by buyers for reference on colour, trimmings and specification sheets.
- The *blue* copy is sent to the Head Office with relevant Kimball (security tags) request sheets.

The buyer creates trend boards showing key silhouettes, prints and colour for a season, along with styling ideas. The trend boards, shop reports and previous sales history, aid buyers in creating a range plan outlining specific styles, fabrics and prices.

The buyer needs to be aware of psychological and sociological processes. They need to be rational about decisions, be aware of competitors' movements, the season's fashion trends and any commercial potential they hold. Most importantly, they need to know the desires of their particular customer base.

Buyers can travel at least twice a year to collect visual information for shop reports, often accompanied by the designer.

Appointments are made to view suppliers' collections. A range review meeting is then held with the buying director, merchandising controller and all buyers, where alterations to ranges may occur after advice is given.

Orders are then placed and 'sealing' samples of each garment are requested. These are submitted to the garment technician along with a specification sheet including measurements and a technical drawing. A 'fit' meeting between the buyer and technician is held to look at the garment fit on a model and the garment is then either approved or if amended a second sealing sample is requested.

When the garment is fully approved and sealed it can then be put into production. The production sample is then measured by the assistant or garment technologist against the original sealing specification sheet. Washing, care and fabric content and laboratory dips are also checked before the sample is approved. Samples not approved can result in orders being cancelled at the buyer's request.

Each week a list of the best sellers is compiled for each store. This involves consulting on stock, sales and any other information to define the best selling lines.

THE FUNCTION OF THE BUYER

Fashion Careers – Assistant Designer High Street

Large department stores often employ design teams to work on their own ranges. Each designer in the team is allocated a design assistant, who is trained to think about the detail regarding a particular label. They can assist with any colour and fabric sourcing. They may also be asked to do any necessary computer-aided design (CAD) work.

General duties for a design assistant could be photocopying, ordering stationery and preparing trend and range boards for meetings.

Each designer is in charge of one, two or even three different ranges. The duties involved are many – primarily design, leading on to colour and fabric sourcing for each range.

The designers work closely with buyers on a day-to-day basis, re-draughting garments when required and often accompanying the buyers and merchandisers on visits to the supplier.

The designer needs to know about new trends and requires information from fashion magazines, shop windows, merchandise inside shops, prediction publications, the Internet, the changing consumer and street style.

A series of trend boards are then compiled, each with a different theme, including emerging or current trends, along with written information pertaining to the visuals.

General duties of the assistant can be:

- Gathering market research.
- Initial sketching of ideas.
- Liaising with the colourist to create a colour palette.
- Using trend information.
- Sourcing fabrics from different suppliers.
- Sourcing trims such as zips and sequins.
- Sketching working drawings.
- Amending any design problems.

Design projects may entail designing ranges for a season a year in advance and would be based around trends researched for that season. Such designs would be circulated amongst the design department and management team in the form of a trend report for use as inspiration and guidance.

Some designs may be developed from this for other labels within the design department. This could result in designing four stories, consisting of an initial 50 garments in each story and working closely with the buyer to create a colour and fabric story.

Trade shows like 40 degrees are visited for their accent on casualwear and streetwear – the best emerging styles and details are noted.

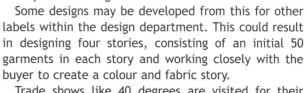

DESIGNER FOR IN-HOUSE LABEL

Fashion Careers – Assistant Designer

The assistant, within a small, designer-level company, requires abilities such as communicating in a professional manner and good organisational skills.

Design and confidence improve whilst constantly dealing with strict deadlines and budgets which require perseverance and discipline. International links can mean different cultures working together, language barriers have to be overcome, and social skills and working relationships with manufacturers, suppliers and other designers develop.

Colour palettes are produced each season. Initially they are extensive but subsequent design meetings reduce the palette down to a more manageable size. Past seasons' sales figures are reviewed to produce a list of the most popular colourways.

Initial design meetings involve looking at trend information for the coming seasons and catwalk designers. From this information, the design team are able to develop a brief and produce mood boards that create a strong theme. At all times the brand image and philosophy are considered. All aspects of the range are discussed – design, print, price points and fabric possibilities – involving the entire team.

FROM INITIAL CONCEPT

Approximately 80 designs may be chosen which will have to be drawn up as specification sheets. These sheets become vital reference documents during production.

After co-ordinating the range, patterns are created for each design. Slight alterations to existing blocks from previous seasons could be carried out by the assistant.

All sample garments may be produced in-house by a sample machinist or at the production factory. These garments are then tried for fit, look, fabric performance and overall garment details. Any necessary changes are added and copies are produced for the sales team.

All measurements have to be exact within a small margin to those on the specification sheet, the branding positioned accurately and any fabric faults noted. A list is then sent to the factories with each garment for reference during production. The samples produced in-house are then allocated a factory and sent with their pattern, specification sheets and garment notes.

Assistants may be required to source new manufacturers. They would need to find out about: the smallest quantities possible to produce, sample ordering, examples of colourways and costing sheets.

Using the colour cards and product plans (notes regarding fabrics, price points and factories), the designer would attend fabric fairs collecting fabric swatches and ordering sample lengths. The fairs visited twice a year would be Premiere Vision in Paris, and Prato Expo and Moda In in Italy.

The assistant would establish a filing system for the swatches. The swatches gathered from the trips would be used for ordering sample lengths or archived for future reference.

Fashion Careers – Assistant Designer

Whilst the sample collection is being produced at the various factories, sample books are made for the sales team. These are used as a reference for garment information when clients are placing orders. The books contain specification sheets, fabric content and swatches, colourways, sizes, description and country of manufacture. These books are distributed with the sample collection to the sales team. The whole design team will help to produce the books with approximately four colourways for each design.

Garments cannot go into production until a level of sales can be gauged. Some garments and colourways will not gain enough orders and will be dropped from the collection.

As soon as the sales team have completed their task, fabrics and trims are ordered. The assistant has to be sure that suppliers can produce the required quantities within the given schedule and has to constantly chase their progress and allow extra time for any problems. They work between the trim supplier and the garment manufacturer who are waiting for their delivery.

The assistant's role could involve dealing with public relations and advertising – magazines may wish to use the collection. Garments need to be photographed; images need to be delivered in good condition and the assistant needs to meet deadlines for publication.

Point of sale is another task allocated to the assistant involving designing anything from Christmas cards to invitations to showroom displays to boards and postcards to stands on counters.

The assistant may be asked to complete such diverse assignments as designing the garment care and contents labels to styling the new season's brochure. The brief may contain such parameters as small format to save on postage, a fun and quirky image.

The job would entail deciding on a concept, sourcing location and models, the styling at the photo shoot, choosing the photographs and mocking up the brochure.

Production involves liaising with the printers and ensuring that progress is checked for problems and queries so that the brochures can be distributed in time to gain maximum exposure.

Consultancy forms an important part of the business. Companies would approach with a problem(s) and the design team would set out to solve it/them. The client may have such problems as a lack of seasonal co-ordination, poor visual merchandising and confusing point of sale material. The solution would be to provide new design, co-ordination and simplification through the use of more succinct colour stories, balanced range plans, clear messages within showroom displays and good visual merchandising.

Fashion Careers – Visual Merchandising

Retailing has had to look carefully at how it maintains and attracts consumers. The Internet has become a competitor to retailers in that consumers can select and purchase products from home or work, effectively cutting out the effort involved in shopping – parking, amusing the children, finding the time and energy to browse in a society where time is precious.

In the retail sector there are the 'pile them high, sell them cheap' retailers who sell at bargain prices and offer value-for-money shopping experiences. Then there are the 'retail experiences' – retailers who attempt to make the whole experience memorable and enjoyable and hopefully repeatable.

New retail developments may take place in a variety of locations – old abandoned warehouses, defunct factories, urban environments, anywhere that is no longer 'out of town' but is interesting and fresh in concept to entertain an increasingly blasé consumer.

It is necessary to preserve the 'surprise' factor in retail design and visual merchandising. The visual merchandiser needs to understand trends in products and consumer expectations. Their job requires them to work with window displays, table dressing and bust forms. They also need to consider placement of gondolas (display stands) for maximum sales and combine these with other visuals such as photographic styling.

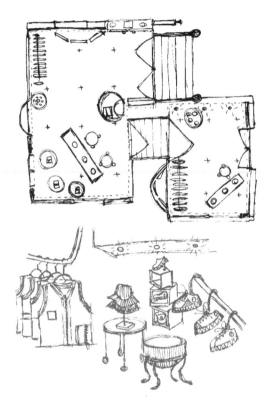

It is important to create an ambience, using light, sound, smell, touch and temperature that will be comfortable to the target markets. The product needs to be perceived by the consumer as indispensable and priced accordingly. There also needs to be enough variation to allow the consumer to feel that they can add their own personality to their purchases. They do not necessarily buy a whole co-ordinated range but mix and match from other brands.

The 'independent' retail space must evoke the 'brand' and communicate clearly the particular message of that brand. Focusing on the brand's philosophy rather than targeting one particular type of consumer avoids alienating consumers. This allows for 'individualism' where each consumer interprets the merchandise differently depending upon their own circumstances. Photographic styling images can be used to imply a mood, by considering layout, image manipulation, cropping and individual detail. Above all, monotony is to be avoided and visual merchandising units are regularly changed to fit with the equally regularly renewed collections. Suppliers of branded goods to a large chain store, for example, would provide fixtures and fittings that echo the philosophy of a brand, and offer advice to sales staff regarding that philosophy.

The aim of the visual merchandiser is to see that the correct merchandise is in the correct place at the correct time, reflecting the correct quality at the correct price!

Fashion Careers – Visual Merchandising

The first impression a customer has of any store is not necessarily the merchandise contained within the store, but the presentation of the window display. It is in this area that the display department plays one of its most important roles.

The larger the retailer's window the more opportunity for projecting a strong concept or theme to the public. Major retailers in London pride themselves on their window displays which can become almost like 'installations' and inspire the consumer to take a look inside the store. Designing the window will take place at Head Office; photographs of the proposed windows will be supplied to retailers, it will reflect the *Zeitgeist* (spirit of the time).

Training programmes highlight the importance of presenting stock in a uniform manner and make employees more aware of themes and the statements that the company wishes to promote nationally, including the reinforcement of any branding.

There is usually a checklist of tasks to consider:

- Consult and discuss stock with managers.
- Check that the correct size is used.
- Select the stock with the best appearance.
- Check the selection for any flaws or faults.
- Check the availability of the stock.

Every time that new garments arrive at the retailer's store this is called a phase. This happens every 6 to 8 weeks. There can be four phases in a season and windows will change about every 3 weeks using at least two types of window for each phase. Display inside the store is also considered; the placement of certain items is crucial to maintaining or building on sales. All aspects of display, including graphics, are considered carefully to maintain the correct image for the store.

The choice of window used depends upon the location of the store and the type of customer who shops there. The display teams put together the window presentation packs and they need to continually update each window in each store so that the look in the window matches that of the photographs in the pack.

DRESSING THE WINDOWS

All garments to be displayed have to be perfectly pressed. Blouses and shirts have to be checked, to see that buttons run down the centre of the display bust. Collars and shoulders need to sit horizontally and be even, crisp and clean. Fabric has to appear as if it has 'life' and not be overworked. Shorts, skirts and jackets are all worked in the same way, checking that they hang squarely on the busts. Pins are used to enhance the fit of the garments and maintain a high-quality finish to the display. Main points to consider are:

- A good balance of colour use.
- A mix of item lengths.
- A mix of hem lengths.

Fashion Careers – Costume Designer

THE COSTUME DESIGNER

Television companies involved in the production of programmes will often have their own costume department which is run as a discrete business. The costume store will house all of the stock, the offices and the workrooms. Hiring-out of costumes to television, advertising, film or theatre productions may be used to generate income.

The costumes are stored in the stockroom. Typically one level is laid out in decades, starting with the present-day clothing for men and women going back to 1940, including a section of shoes and accessories, hats, bags, ties and scarves.

A second level may incorporate period costume dating from 1939 back to medieval dress, including the underwear and accessories for each era, enabling exact details to be reproduced for total authenticity. There are also costumes for light entertainment shows and fantasy dress such as leotards and dancewear, animal suits, science fiction creations and sportswear, uniforms for school, clubs and workwear.

All stock must be booked out on the computer. Once the item is returned it is booked back in and then the stock is put away.

The permanent staff at the store include designers, costumiers, dressers, wardrobe assistants, sewing technicians and clerical staff.

Alterations and new garments are created in the workroom within the store. Sketches are used to create very detailed garments. Designers are expected to work within a budget that is decided by the producer of a show. The size of the budget depends on the popularity, the type of show and the length of the series. Costume dramas will have a larger budget than a contemporary comedy.

The designers are allocated television programmes. Costumiers are employed to support the designer and to ensure the store is utilised to its full potential. With an extensive knowledge of costume and dress, past and present, they can advise designers and outside clients on the availability of items.

Wardrobe assistants help to return 'dead' stock to the correct place and they operate the computer system. They will also assist designers working on a show. The designer may choose how many assistants they require and freelance assistants are often used.

The designer splits the budget into shows and works out how much can be spent on assistants, hire of costumes, buying of costumes and accessories and the cost of having them specially made.

Designers store their own equipment (which has been collected over time) and items bought for shows can be saved and used again, e.g. safety pins, jewellery, shoe polish, toupee tape.

Fashion Careers – Costume Designer

On a typical television programme, that is part of a series, the designer may have to provide costumes for presenters. The presenters will require a different outfit for each programme with an individual identity, yet keep within the designer's ideas. Designer and presenter will shop together to create a wardrobe for the series. The presenters may buy their costumes once the series has finished and can borrow them for personal appearances during the series.

If there is a dance routine within a show, the designer must watch the initial routine for ideas and, once the choreographer and make-up designer have discussed their thoughts, a more accurate idea is formed.

The designer needs to know a script in advance to make provision for scenes.

When dressing older members of a cast, the designer may choose clothes that date back at least 10 years for authenticity. Pensioners do not tend to wear up-to-the-minute clothing; their wardrobe will have been collected from a few decades. This applies to period costume as well as modern day. A library of reference books is available in the costume store to check such details.

When filming away from the studio, more planning is necessary, depending on the distance from the costume store. All of the costumes are transported on the correct rails to the location. The designer may accompany the crew if the location is abroad. Everything must be recorded and labelled before leaving the store as there is a greater chance of losing costumes on location.

If a scene has to be filmed more than once, and a costume may be soaked as part of the drama, duplicates will need to be provided. The designers must also pay for the use of the studio laundry.

The visual effects department may also work with the designer. The designer can create an image on paper and the visual effects team will make it. They are responsible for producing believable effects with the minimum of danger.

Although costume design is not directly related to fashion design it is a career that incorporates the same design skills and, at the same time, requires a broad knowledge of both historical costume and contemporary fashion.

Fashion Careers – Working for a Magazine

Magazines usually work 3 months ahead of the time that the magazine is published to ensure that there is enough time for research, the photo shoot, the addition of text, passing through the art department, passing to the sub-editors and then to the editor who approves the pages before production.

The fashion assistant will have a variety of roles and responsibilities at the magazine, not least the role of stylist.

The stylist, nowadays, has a much broader remit than in the past. Styling can be about fashion meeting other disciplines – setting up photographic shoots to provide visuals for interiors, food, popular music, trend and lifestyle publications (lifestyle is the consideration of all aspects of design that affect our daily lives, all of the functioning products that we use or enjoy, that entertain or enhance our lives, for example interior products, designer fridges and kettles, not just clothing).

The magazine stylist may show their versatility by taking work in television and cinema by transference of their skills to moving media.

The magazine fashion department could consist of fashion director, senior fashion editor and a fashion assistant. The fashion director produces the main fashion story each month. The director has to ensure that the stories match the priorities of the magazine's target audience in terms of style, age and budget.

The features that will be followed are discussed with the editor and fashion director together with the rest of the team. Staff are assigned to certain projects and the budget available is allocated. The expenses are for models, photographer, location, transport and food. The clothing can be shot on models or as flats.

The fashion department may be allocated as many as 30 pages approximately for each edition which would consist of two fashion stories and a 'Best Buys' page, for example. The two fashion stories are made up of photographic images. Each story normally would follow one of the main trends for a season. The best buys would show a number of trends.

For a high summer issue the magazine may use a larger budget to shoot abroad ensuring good weather around April or May. The senior fashion editor may produce the second fashion story following the director's and editor's criteria.

The fashion assistant would take it in turn to work with the fashion director or senior fashion editor and can also pursue shoots alone. The assistant needs to be fully aware of what the director and editor are doing on their shoots and could be called to take over at any moment.

Good contacts with public relations (PR) companies are essential when borrowing garments.

Fashion Careers – Working for a Magazine

The briefing informs all involved regarding the trend/story that is to be followed. The type of clothing needed is discussed. Research will have to be undertaken about the clothes that are of potential use for a story and where the garments may be located.

The location of a shoot could be Britain or abroad, or it could be in a studio. Studios will charge a reasonable fee or may be free. Dates should be booked and recorded in a diary.

The photographer is booked from a list after liaising with the art department about the type of shots required.

The models are selected from model agencies by portfolio, and final castings are made where the models try on the garments.

Clothing is loaned out on the condition that full credit is given in the magazine including stockists, designer and price.

Public relations (PR) companies and in-house public relations hold one or more brands of clothing with a view to getting the newest ranges publicised for their clients. They may be contacted to organise the borrowing of the clothes and when they would be returned. It is possible to visit their showrooms, with an appointment or on press days, and look at samples that may be relevant to a shoot.

All samples are stored on rails at the magazine and the assistant is responsible for systematically labelling and filing the garments carefully to facilitate easy return to the PR companies. Once all garments are received for a shoot the 'styling' of outfits is begun (accessorising an outfit and deciding on hairstyles and make-up). The day before the shoot the garments need bagging up and labelling with the location address.

Once at the shoot some garments may need pressing and extra garments would be always included to cover unforeseen problems.

As the shoot progresses a note is made of which garments have been used, the stockists and price. At the end of the shoot all garments are replaced in their bags for an easy return to the PR company.

All documentation of the borrowed garments and of returning the garments is meticulously kept as proof of delivery back to the PR companies.

The day after a shoot the proofs are returned to the magazine so that the final shots can be chosen and the text and credits added. This is then passed to the editor for approval and then is passed to the art department for final alterations before production.

Within two months the magazine is on the shelves!

Fashion Careers – Fashion Predictor

FASHION PREDICTION CONSULTANTS

Fashion prediction companies, or fashion forecasters as they are also known, tend to be fairly small publishing enterprises. They may have core design staff dealing with any artwork and core administrative staff dealing with the business side including accounts, salaries and general office duties.

The process of fashion forecasting follows a pattern which leads to the creation of commercial, forward-looking publications in the form of limited edition books with fashion themes for the coming seasons.

The core design staff will have their own area of expertise and are responsible for the artwork which will be used in the prediction publications and in any consultancy undertaken. The personnel may be menswear, womenswear or childrenswear designers, colour consultants, textile consultants or graphic designers.

Freelancers are hired to bring in an area of knowledge or expertise not catered for already by the core staff. For example an experienced womenswear designer may be employed for a consultancy project where knowledge of a particular market is required, or a knitwear freelancer may be used to produce forward-thinking samples for a publication. Alternatively, a freelancer may be employed to produce work that a core member is capable of doing, but due to work load has insufficient time to do so.

Core staff are responsible for all initial ideas and decisions on colours, fabrics and theme directions, and guide all support staff in their roles. The publication will have a very distinctive style of its own and all employees will be expected to comply with this.

Students are generally hired to carry out the menial but time-consuming work which needs to be done for every project, for example finding images for theme boards by looking at numerous magazines, or photocopying work as a record for the company. However, students need to learn and after proving themselves responsible will be allowed more creative projects.

Due to the frequent turn-over of books and consultancy projects, design staff need to be aware of declining trends and growing undercurrents in fashion. A large number of national and international magazines are read each month, as well as an interest taken in current movements in film, music, theatre, art and any other cultural activities.

Developments in fabrics are keenly awaited due to their direct effect on fashion and clothing. Design staff will visit all of the European fashion and fabric fairs.

144

Fashion Careers – Product Development

The product development assistant is expected to assist in developing all aspects of the production cycle from design development through to quality control before launching the product.

The cycle begins when the retailer being supplied releases their 'Critical Path' to suppliers. This is a guide to all dates and deadlines that the suppliers must meet. It also contains presentation and meeting dates for the following months ahead to ensure that the product will be produced and distributed to stores ready for the range launch date.

Once the supplier is given a design brief from the retailer, research on the product can begin.

A 'strategy meeting' is then arranged by the supplier who will include such information for the product as:

1. Comparative and directional shopping looking at merchandise in the high street and designer sectors, comparing pieces by price, fabrication, quality (comparative), and also looking at inspirational merchandise for direction and emerging new trends (directional).

2. Samples of merchandise purchased to take back to the suppliers for further investigation.

Specific information required for reports would be the product type, price points, fabric/fibre content, colour and a description of the product including special style features.

The department manager and fabric technologist will visit fabric and yarn shows such as Premiere Vision and Pitti Filati. Here samples of yarns and fabrics are selected and ordered, and will be presented to the retailer in the first presentation a few months away.

THE CRITICAL PATH

145

Fashion Careers – Product Development

The manufacturers are controlled by the suppliers and retailers using a White Seal Standard. This includes requirements such as the quality of the product (every garment or item must be the same), the size, colour, fabrication and style.

A pre-meeting is held between the product area manager and the director. This is held after completing research work and comparative shopping, and is called to decide which bought samples and design ideas should be shown to the retailer in the strategy meeting.

Current trends (high street and designer), historical sales (what was previously a good seller in store), and price points (dictated by the retailer) are all reviewed; the merchandisers are consulted (they decide what the company can afford). The strategy meeting is then held and is followed up by preparation for the concept product meeting. The presentation here will include key shapes, designs and fabrics, technical priorities and innovations.

The controls that affect the supplier are: what is affordable for them (for example, what is the quality of yarn that can be afforded?), the merchandisers, personal opinions from the retailer, price points and seasonal colour palettes provided by the retailer.

SUPPLIERS AND SOURCING

All yarn and fabric sourcing is often carried out at the yarn shows and from overseas suppliers.

In the textiles division the garment has to be produced from start to finish, sourcing and selecting yarns in the correct weight and colour.

Factories may be situated in a completely different country to the fabric source and therefore lead times need to be taken into account to manufacture and ship to the United Kingdom in time for the product launch.

The assistant will also need to produce specification drawings for the manufacturer to use in sampling. These drawings need to be accurate interpretations of the design so that they can be translated exactly into the product required and include measurements to guide the manufacturer.

Communicating with the factories is part of the assistant's job and at times this can be difficult due to language problems and time differences.

When the samples finally arrive they are inspected and decisions regarding modifications are made. The manufacturer is informed of any changes prior to resubmission.

The products are all tagged with the supplier's label for the meeting with the retailer so that they are not confused with other suppliers' products.

Fashion Careers – Product Development

Whilst the product development is progressing, packaging is also being developed. The retailer will give a packaging brief to the supplier.

The assistant will produce mood boards, design development boards and presentation boards for meetings and presentations. For the concept product meeting, design development boards and style boards are prepared to support the sample developments in the meeting.

The final presentation is the presentation where all samples are displayed amongst mood boards in the presentation room. The ambience of the room must set the scene for the meeting. This is a crucial meeting, and everything has to be perfect as the retailer will make final decisions about the products that they wish to go into production.

When the retailer has made their decision they inform the supplier of any changes they require and then the supplier sets to work on arranging the White Seal samples for the final product meeting – Phase 1. This meeting includes final White Seal samples, which are presented in the correct colours and fabrics, with full technical specifications and costings agreed.

At production the technologist, aided by the assistant, make quality control checks to ensure that the product meets the correct standard. Three of the best samples will be selected as the White Seal samples and will be tagged detailing the supplier name, the product number and the date of the final product meeting. The supplier will place orders with manufacturers for the required amount of product guided by the retailer – the Green Seal product. A meeting is held with the retailer to ensure that the quality of the product is correct and is of an agreed standard. If the final product does not reach the agreed standard then it will have an RTM (which means return to manufacturer) and leads to the supplier losing a great deal of money.

An order will be placed for packaging at this point. When the samples of packaging and labels arrive at the supplier the product needs to be packed ready for the Green Seal meeting with packaging. The meeting is held with the retailer and Green Seal tags are signed if the retailer is happy with the way the packed product looks. The retailer then gives the go-ahead for production.

At this stage bulk production is flowing through to keep stores in stock. Being aware of lead times for a possible repeat order is essential if stock is selling well.

Any technical issues that are raised either by the retailer or unsatisfied customers, including returned goods, has to be dealt with in the supplier's technical department and often by the assistant.

Fashion Careers – Textile Agent

TEXTILE AGENTS REPRESENTING TEXTILE MILLS

A textile collection begins one year before being seen by the public.

Prediction information is gathered from prediction agencies; designer catwalk collections and high street collections are researched. The textile agent sells the collection on behalf of the textile mill – they will have agents in a variety of countries.

A printed textile mill may release 30 new print designs in each collection. Colour combinations are produced before final decisions, regarding colour, are made. Final designs are chosen and screens are created to begin the printing process. The greater the number of colours involved the more expensive it is to produce the print. An eight-colour print can cost £2000 to create. Mills design textile prints and also buy them in. The current cost (2001) is about £300 per design.

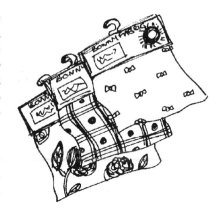

Colours can be altered to match retailers' colour palettes and print mock-ups made by computer-aided design (CAD) for the customer to see. This is all done by the agents in each country to allow the mill to run smoothly.

Fabric orders are booked and delivery is negotiated. Large deliveries of printed cloth can take up to 4 weeks. Base fabrics depend upon the needs of the customer. After confirming an order the base 'grey goods'(undyed cloth) are booked for dyeing on approval of colour. Strike-offs (small pieces of grey goods) are printed to the customer's colours and submitted to the manufacturer for approval. The colour is confirmed through the agent and the mill can then go ahead with the dyeing, printing and finishing. Prints can use 'print on' or 'discharge' techniques.

MILLS AND THE DESIGN PROCESS

The fabric finishes are chemicals that can change the handle or soften the cloth. The fabric is rolled into pieces 50 metres long and sectioned into colour batches – these are different colour batches that are made every time the printer has to re-mix the dyestuffs used to print the cloth. Although the same colour is being produced there can be slight variations in colour that must be noted for the manufacturer's reference. A packing list is produced cataloguing every piece number and the colour batch to which it belongs. This is sent to the agent along with a cutting of each batch and will be shown to the manufacturer for approval. The factory can then arrange to cut the batches in separate lays.

Premiere Vision is the major fabric fair for the fashion and textile industry. Buyers and manufacturers view thousands of different textile ranges under one roof. Agents make sales appointments with customers.

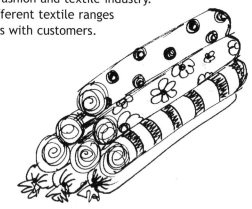

Bulk fabric leaves the mill and is monitored by the agency until it reaches the delivery destination. Anything from outside the European Union requires customs forms. Goods transported to the United Kingdom are delivered to the agent's approved carrier until the manufacturer gives a 'call-off' address.

After-sales communication is dealt with by the agency, for example any problems and repeat orders.

Fashion Careers – Recruitment Consultant

The fashion recruitment consultant broadly deals with the areas of menswear, womenswear and childrenswear design. They also deal with specialist areas such as lingerie, accessories, textiles, knitwear, homeware and activewear.

'Non'-design areas for recruitment are production, illustration, product development, retail, visual display, merchandising, sales, graphics, forecasting, buying, quality control, pattern cutting and administration. Permanent jobs cover all levels from junior right through to senior and director positions.

Consultants need to be well informed regarding changes and trends in the fashion industry. They need to be aware of the latest fashion graduates, the curriculum content of the courses, the best degree shows. They also need to know who is designing for which fashion house, which companies are facing closure, and what's new on the catwalks.

They also need to be aware of the trade press, to attend catwalk shows and fashion fairs. They need to subscribe to most of the trade journals, for example *Drapers Record*, *Womenswear Daily*, *International Textiles*, *Collezioni series*, *The Diary*, *Womenswear Buyer*. Each consultant needs to be responsible for reading as many of these as possible. Extensive travel through Europe is required to attend shows and fairs, for example Pitti Filati in Florence and Premiere Vision in Paris. It is also necessary to meet clients at these venues and search for new ones.

A recruitment consultant has a demanding job. Many prestigious fashion companies are dealt with and this requires patience, sensitivity, perseverance, excellent communication skills, negotiation skills and a 'passion for fashion'.

The client is the source of income, not the candidate. The consultant looks at all levels of every market and sector – manufacturing, retailing, design house, high street, middle market, designer, ready to wear, couture.

The agency has to deal with new university graduates through to managing directors, who have been in the business for many years. Candidates need an extensive portfolio of personal work – hand drawn, for example specification drawings and flatwork, illustration and figure drawings, anything that shows their capabilities in their specialist area. Candidates need a wide range of ideas, clear flatwork, evidence of good use of colour, fabric and printed textiles. The candidate needs to be open to constructive criticism, willing to talk about their ideas, work openly and clearly, and have a good attitude to the recruitment process.

Candidates fill out a registration form, including all relevant information such as education and previous employer. The consultant needs to build up a summary of each individual who it is expected will stay with the agency throughout their career.

DESIGN AND NON-DESIGN

Fashion Careers – New Media Promotion

NEW MEDIA DESIGNERS

There are now design careers in a variety of areas. These can include: promotions for television and advertising, for example conceptual costume design reflecting the seasons, to introduce elements such as the weather; Internet design, for example innovative, interactive web sites promoting and selling clothing brands on-line; CD-ROMs/DVD, for example offering more in-depth interactive information regarding a magazine's contents, or delivering information in the form of interactive entertainment, education or conceptual thinking; kiosks at trade fairs, for example interactive fashion prediction trends, adding depth to a traditionally two-dimensional medium; presentational and promotional video, for example a film that delivers a new concept, or series of new trends visually and with the power of audio.

This is a complex industry with many approaches under the 'new media' umbrella and whilst this could be daunting to a designer, it must be acknowledged that 'team work' plays an important part and it is possible to learn from contemporaries in these situations.

Whatever the medium it is important to be able to communicate clearly to clients. If they can't understand what your business is about how can they be sure that you can communicate what they require? New media companies require fluent business and marketing strategies as well as fluency in 'new media' speak.

Design ideas can be sold successfully by using new media presentation skills. Working with a client, after thorough research and preparation, is key to communicating ideas. Numerous techniques can be applied to bring concepts to life, for example interactive projects authored using Macromedia Director, slide presentations using Microsoft Powerpoint, explanatory videos using Adobe Premiere and After Effects; all have sophisticated visual outputs that can make a difference when selling ideas.

VIDEO AND ON-LINE PUBLICATIONS

Some web design companies may contract out work and the client needs to be sure that there will be long-term, ongoing support once the initial project has been completed.

New media companies need to listen and learn from their clients as well as presenting themselves with confidence. They need to understand thoroughly the client's market and aims.

Fashion Careers – New Media Promotion

Glossy presentation is no substitute for good ideas. These have to be communicated clearly to the client. New ways of thinking are needed to maintain the consumer's interest. Targeting markets and being able to understand their needs implicitly is crucial to all design disciplines. Branding remains an important issue for product manufacturers and service providers. New media is a perfect vehicle for communicating brands and marketing to particular niche markets, for example via the Internet or on CD-ROMs in market-orientated magazines and giveaways.

Different disciplines in design now cross over into other territories, encouraging new ways of thinking; for example, a three-dimensional furniture designer could be included in ideas generation for a fashion product. They will bring with them fresh approaches, with less preconceived ideas.

Similarly, new media is a tool that can be used by any discipline to communicate to clients. New media designers need to keep abreast of rapid change and be a good judge of which innovations are worth pursuing and which are not until they have been proven worthy.

One of the advantages of the Internet is the fact that it can be updated easily and regularly; this could prove to be a bonus for the fashion industry which regularly introduces new ranges seasonally and inter-seasonally. Selling from a website is becoming a popular option for branded clothing lines. It is easy for loyal customers to find company websites with search facilities. It is also easy to find like-minded sites using the same facility and thereby broadening the choice of the consumer. The disadvantage of using the Internet is that garments cannot be handled and delivery times can be long. Mail order catalogues tend to have speedier delivery times, although Internet companies are improving this aspect of their service.

An emphasis on technology and software has been overtaken by a need for 'brand' knowledge, business and management skills, and innovative conceptual thinking, as in all areas of design. Now that the initial Internet investment 'rush' has settled down, companies can concentrate on building stable businesses.

Fashion Careers – Supplier

Buyers rarely deal directly with manufacturers, preferring to buy their merchandise through a reliable and trusted agent or through a third party known as a supplier.

Suppliers may work with two separate ranges: their own label range sold through their own shops or wholesaled to sell through small independent outlets; and designs specifically undertaken for high street chains, for example Top Shop, Miss Selfridge and Wallis. Manufacture may take place domestically or abroad dependent upon cost-effectiveness or particular skills required that are available in a particular part of the world. This would require the supplier to travel frequently to 'source' garments, fabrics, trims or anything else required for the production process.

All supply personnel work closely together to maintain specified delivery dates given by the buyers who work to a strict calender. Delay in the supplying of an order can result in costly last-minute cancellations by the buyer.

Being involved in the supply chain is a challenging yet rewarding career, which offers scope for long-term professional relationships with buying personnel and the chance to travel to and be involved in buying meetings.

Supply firms are, in the main, responsible for the design, sampling, costing, selling, production, shipment, finishing and delivery of goods to the buyer's store. Therefore, within this sector of the fashion industry, lie many job opportunities such as design, production, marketing, as well as the liaising with the buyers and managing their orders under the role of account executive.

The 'supplier' career is very similar to the product development career. Much greater detail is explored in the product development career.

SUPPLIER TO BUYER

Case Study – Introduction

The Case Study is designed to show key points that lie within the body of the book. It is not definitive but follows the design process. It begins with a brief followed by a 'personal philosophy' to give some explanation about the thought process and approach to the subject. Certain parameters have to be set to be able to make design decisions. The process becomes an enjoyable exploration and personal expression that fits the brief.

There were **no** preconceived ideas about how this project would develop and conclude. The work shown is expected to provide a reasonable quantity of development to achieve the desired creativity. Each element could easily be greatly elaborated upon.

THE BRIEF

Consumer attitudes* are divided. On the one hand the whole world is at our fingertips and the Internet allows access to vast amounts of information at the speed of a mouse click. Nowadays we have a much better understanding and awareness of global issues. On the other hand, consumers want to keep in touch with 'planet earth', with an adverse reaction to cyberspace, media overload and political hype; they are looking back to a slower pace of life, of past generations and are reviving interest in country pursuits, such as walking, riding, and picnicking.

Bear this in mind and design a small womenswear collection for Autumn/Winter 2001/2002. The collection should cover all major items and any directional pieces deemed necessary to make the collection special, desirable, fresh and new.

The collection will be sold in designer-level boutiques and will be primarily aimed at working women aged 25-45. There is an opportunity to develop a collection of childrenswear also using a similar 'lifestyle' brief.

This is a new venture and also requires some promotional information such as a corporate identity for the company and relevant graphics. Any marketing ideas would also be useful.

KATHRYN McKELVEY'S PERSONAL DESIGN PHILOSOPHY

- To produce *versatile* clothing that can be worn for work and dressed up for more formal occasions, for leisure and weekend wear – achieved by using accessories and *layering* for different looks.
- A literal interpretation of themes is not desired, but a look with *many influences subtly interwoven* into the design. Some basic pieces, some fun pieces, some interesting construction pieces.
- *Practical* clothing, not too feminine, but with the odd feminine detail to attract a broader range of consumer.
- With an interest in *construction* and adding volume as a key direction at this time. How can this be done in a more inventive way?
- Clothing that is comfortable but with added *freshness*, is *beautiful* and *aesthetically pleasing*, with attention to detail but a *dramatic silhouette*.
- Modern, *lots of texture* and *pattern mixed* together but the colour would be controlled, for example *tone on tone* to give some order; the design needs logic.
- Showing the designs on the figure allows experimentation with colour, print, pattern, scale and texture; also to test out 'the look' in terms of proportion.
- What sort of shapes are dramatic yet practical? Does the designing move away from the original idea? Is that good? A great variety of research materials – spark off many channels and ideas. Is there enough fashion input? Does it hang together? Ideas are tested out on paper – they then need to be tested in three dimensions. Ideas are still developing when moved to the next medium, namely the pattern and the toile.

*Consumer attitudes courtesy of Worth Global Style Network.

Case Study – Introduction

The research began with a favourite book about Tibet, one that had been sitting on a shelf for 2 years waiting ... Another book called *(Un)Fashion* (Tibor & Kalman, 2000) seemed the perfect antithesis for a book about designing for fashion.

The *Fashion Source Book* (McKelvey, 1996) was used for interesting garment construction, and current lifestyle books were consulted for the quirky and unusual. The research took on an eclectic, ethnic flavour. Colour work was derived from the book on Tibet and 'the natural' in the lifestyle books.

A contemporary exhibition on children's book illustration provided an opportunity to gather some inspirational text about the human condition and our need to hear stories, whether it be through a bedtime book or a new movie with computer-generated special effects.

RESEARCH DIRECTION

The research direction consisted of looking at fashion prediction material for the correct season. Silhouette, proportion, and garment fit, were all noted as illustrations. Key words were gleaned from the information to give more ideas about garment types, detail, fabrication and trims. Directional designer catwalk collections were reviewed in keeping with the personal philosophy. Favourite designers such as Comme Des Garçons and Yohji Yamamoto were researched – both contemporary and past collections.

RESEARCH DIRECTION – MARKET REFERENCE

Current magazines were reviewed for styling and garment combinations, and key points were noted.

A directional shop report was conducted to find garments of interesting construction, and to note the use of detail, fabric combinations and accessories, either relevant to the market or interesting enough to develop a new direction. As much information as possible was noted on the page.

THE DESIGN PROCESS

A fabric story needed to be constructed to support the design development. Little could be done until there was a firm understanding of which fabrics would be used. Some flexibility is needed, and consequently the fabric development is quite varied.

Fabric development began by looking at textiles in lifestyle books. Textiles were simple and almost of a naïve quality; the work of Janet Bolton came to mind and was duly recorded. Architecture became a focus for printed textile ideas because of the sculptural quality, scale and drama of some buildings. A contrast between naïvety, pattern mixes, checks and stripes, and overwhelming scale was desired. Polyvinyl chloride (PVC) fabrics were useful for creating sculptural shapes. A PVC welder was available to construct garments, so, to achieve the technological dimension mentioned in the brief, sculptural samples were created. The fabric story was also 'worked up' as a colour story and some of these ideas are shown on pages 207–18. The sculptural work was developed in naturals echoing the stone and slate research drawings. Then followed a green and red colour story reflecting colour from the book on Tibet and showing naïve pattern and surface decoration mixes, with a glint of sparkle and shine. Then a return to naturals showed naïve patterns in matt and dry handles, with large-scale knit stitches and matt beading, and surface decoration. The 'swirl' motif, from research, was introduced in a small scale and subsequently in a variety of ways. The PVC welding technique was mixed with naïve patterns and metal foil was introduced primarily for use in accessories. Glass beading was large and chunky; buttons and pigskin were 'whitewashed' for a bleached effect.

Case Study – Introduction

With this variety of fabric stories, design, in the form of silhouette, cut and detail, was begun. The research material was reviewed and drawing of shapes began. A logical process of trying out surface decoration and print ideas was applied to designs to achieve some sort of balance.

DESIGN DEVELOPMENT

Design development began with laying out all of the research material. The research material was reviewed and the key pointers were noted and retained for development. The design development was also laid out on a table as it was being created, to get a full picture of how it was developing.

The fabric story was also close by for reference, all the time; whilst designing, mental notes about the most useful and directional parts of the fabric story were made. It may have helped to actually list key design directions and key fabric directions, as the design process can become something of a 'juggling' exercise.

Drawing is the key tool to developing ideas; it is the simplest way to communicate. Well-informed design requires:

- Good observational skills.
- An awareness of the anatomy of the body.
- An awareness of the drape of fabrics on the body.
- An awareness of the movement of the body.
- An awareness of the potential of garment construction.
- An understanding of individual fabric performance (or an ability to experiment with a new fabric by sampling).

Other tools for designing may be experimenting with paper; for example, one of the skirts in the case study was developed by manipulating four rectangles of paper. Collage can be valuable in creating an impression of an oversized print or pattern. Working directly on a mannequin with a piece of unfinished calico to create a shape (a toile) is a normal method of working directly in three dimensions.

Experience builds on this knowledge and the designer needs to constantly, consciously and subconsciously, add to this data. Sketchbooks are essential for making this sort of notation when the designer has little experience to draw upon. Sketchbook work is also useful to the experienced designer for showing detail and cut that cannot be retained by memory or some sort of inspiration that may not be right for now but could be useful in the future.

Being a designer is not the sort of job that ever ceases; experiences are constantly being evaluated and potentially translated even when travelling, taking a vacation, watching television, looking at magazines and advertising.

Once a variety of design developments have occurred it may be helpful to try out some of the garments together to 'test' the look. Some designers create designs directly on a figure and then develop the finer points, such as fastenings, later. The case study was developed with no preconceived notion of the final 'look'. This made the design journey much more exciting and inspirational. Awareness that there would be strong ethnic influences, but also a strong functional influence, was implicit in the designing.

The illustration of the 'look', including patterns and prints to scale and accessories, gives a good idea of what is expected.

Case Study – Introduction

DESIGN DEVELOPMENT - CHILDRENSWEAR

Once the womenswear look was established, it seemed appropriate to try out the same information on childrenswear, more specifically girlswear. Whilst the basic philosophy translated well and most of the research material would also work, the construction of the garments needed to be curtailed as they became too unwieldy.

Working on babieswear gives slightly more problems in that construction needs to be considered carefully and there are a number of points to take into account such as: no drawstrings around the neck or head (applies to children also) and no small pieces of loose trim that a baby may be able to chew. Other regulations such as flame-retardant nightwear fabrics and basic commonsense design need to be at the forefront when designing for babies.

Designing for children and babies is much easier when you have had the experience of actually caring for them: dressing them; changing nappies; buying shoes, hats and socks that stay on; watching them grow out of clothing. Obviously it is not practical to give birth to children just to design for them, so what is the next best thing? Research is very important, asking the right questions about fit, ease of access for changing nappies without undressing a small baby, practical clothing that stands up to crawling on hard and soft floors, fabrics that will wash again and again without losing quality, for example. Seek out parents, relatives with children or visit play groups and nurseries (telephone for permission first!).

PRINT DEVELOPMENT - CHILDRENSWEAR

Although the basic ideas from the inspiration were considered to be sound, the actual print aspect needed some more work. It was decided to develop some extra figurative print motifs and the obvious ones were 'animals' because of the way children relate to them. They can also be very decorative. After drawing a toy donkey, pig, dog and hippopotamus, the texture of the drawings was pleasing enough to use directly in some print development. The motifs were repeated using computer software in very simplistic 'one-way prints'.

A whole sketchbook of work could be completed very quickly using this process. The only real element missing was the development of colour and colour stories. This would add real dynamism to the print ideas. Also different fabric surfaces would take the print slightly differently, for example printing on a velvet as opposed to a cotton voile.

WORKING DRAWING

Once the paper-based designing came to an end it was time to create some three-dimensional products. But working drawings of the garments intended for development needed to be produced. It was essential to resolve problems such as fastenings and construction, using back, front and side views, if necessary. Decisions were then made regarding placement of details.

Fabric swatches attached to the drawing helped to visualise the final garment and were an aid to understanding how the fabric would behave.

PROTOTYPING

Once the pattern was created, the design was cut out in calico to test the shape and find out any potential problems. The toile produced was placed on the dress stand and it was immediately obvious that it was too long. Other problems were: it was going to be difficult to attach a waistband, consequently a test sample was required to resolve this problem; the zip fastening, and the siting of it, needed to be resolved; also the rectangular construction did not allow for a natural opening in the normal places – centre back, centre front or side seam?

Case Study – Introduction

The concept was interesting so the garment was made up in two contrasting fabrics – a nylon ciré, lightweight and fluid, and a padded waterproof fabric, very rounded and sculptural in structure. Both garments were completely finished to see how the sample would translate.

PROMOTION/GRAPHICS

Now that the product was taking shape the promotional side could be considered. The brief required a 'corporate identity' to be created for this new business venture.

The design process was applied to the graphics aspect. Design development sheets were created with some research ideas included to give direction. A name for the company had to be chosen, so this was logically worked out by using key words from the personal philosophy.

Once the name was chosen and fonts experimented with, the rest of the identity could be executed. The computer certainly becomes invaluable when attempting this sort of exercise.

Close-up digital photographs of flowers were used to introduce pure colour and texture and related well to the project. The identity included letterhead, business cards and promotional postcards. Packaging and gift packaging were included as was a promotional mail order brochure, an extra marketing idea.

PROMOTION/STYLING

The mail order brochure required some photographic styling of garments. These were created hypothetically by using shots of the skirts created in the two different fabrics. Other garment shapes were created also using the illustrations and design development sheets. More styling was needed for poster campaigns.

The process was as before; research material was gathered of contemporary fashion styling and ideas were 'weeded out'. The main problem/challenge was the lack of a model. Would it be possible to create contemporary fashion styling without a model?

There has been a resurgence of interest in fashion illustration recently. This should be seen as a positive way of promoting the collection. Computer software proved invaluable as did the photographs of the prototypes which were superimposed over the illustrations. A very simple and quite stark effect!

The following pages show the visuals produced as the design process progressed. The basic poses (both adult and child) for the sketches were sourced from *Fashion Source Book* (McKelvey, 1996) and *Illustrating Fashion* (McKelvey & Munslow, 1997).

Case Study – Research Inspiration

Tibet

Tibet

shape and cut, pattern and drape

Tibet

Tibet - on the Paths of the Gentlemen Brigands
Tiziana & Gianni Baldizzone

Case Study – Research Inspiration

oil barrel hat

chimney pot hat

stripes

Un-Fashion

shape and cut, pattern and drape

protective, wrapping

Un-Fashion

Un-Fashion

wrapping, protection

white

protective

yellow glasses

Un-Fashion

Case Study – Research Inspiration

pebbles and slate, alpine

broken crockery

mosaics by Kaffe Fassett & Candace Bahouth

colour and pattern

from Eco Deco by Stewart & Sally Walton

stone mosaic

natural colours

shapely sundial

painted stones natural with black

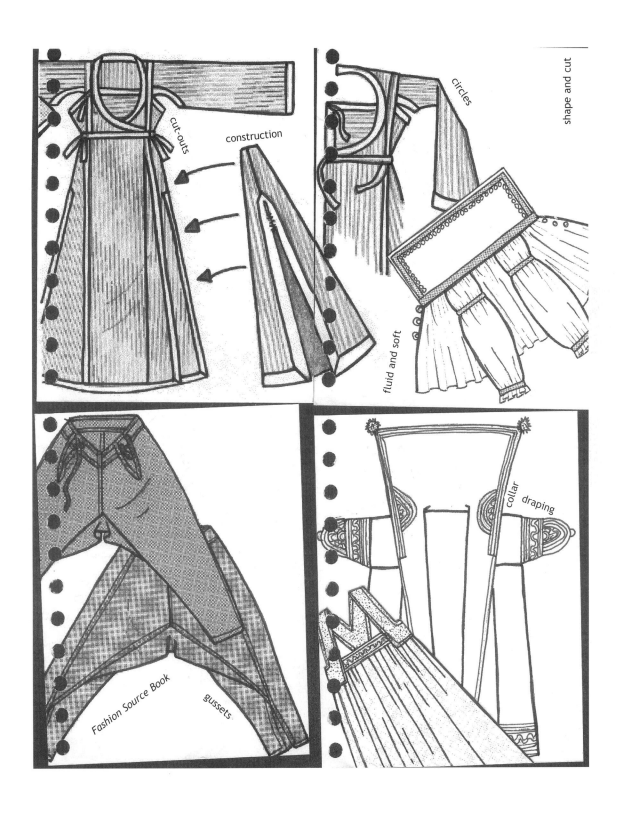

cut-outs

construction

circles

shape and cut

fluid and soft

Fashion Source Book

gussets

collar

draping

Case Study – Research Inspiration

1959 Japanese Calendar

from *Eco Deco* by Stewart & Sally Walton

from *Eco Deco* by Stewart & Sally Walton

pattern and form

Exhibition at Newcastle Arts Centre on Children's Book Illustration

November 2000

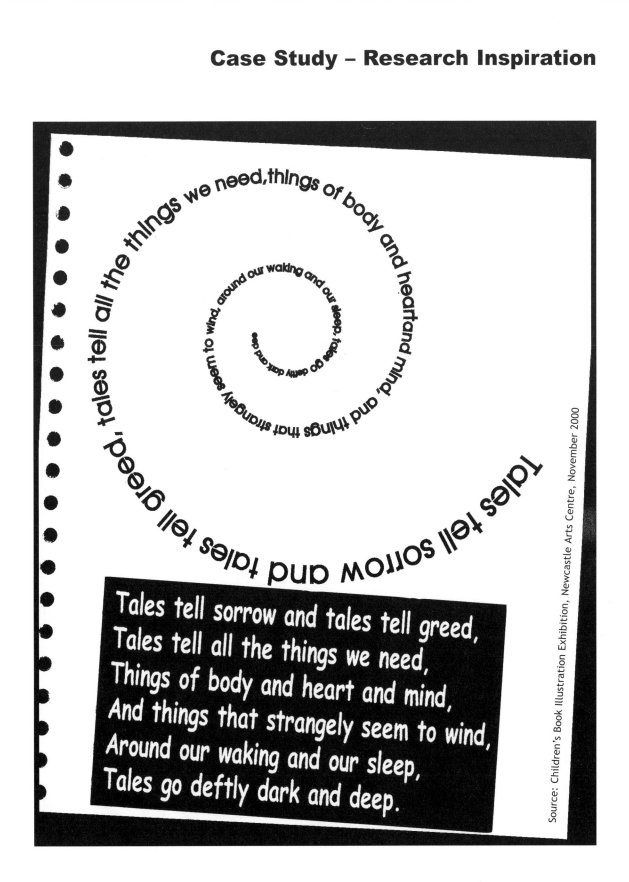

Tales tell sorrow and tales tell greed,
Tales tell all the things we need,
Things of body and heart and mind,
And things that strangely seem to wind,
Around our waking and our sleep,
Tales go deftly dark and deep.

Source: Children's Book Illustration Exhibition, Newcastle Arts Centre, November 2000

Case Study – Research Direction

silhouette direction: Worth Global Style Network

164

Yohji Yamamoto

Yohji Yamamoto

Christian Lacroix

layers

Giorgio Armani

off-the-shoulder

contemporary designers

Shu fabric

Dai Rees

Key words - styling
Autumn/Winter 2001/2002
Worth Global Style Network:
Cape shaped coats/jackets/lay-ered/multi fabric skirts dropped hem under slips knitted tops sep-arate cowl collars volume skirts experimental pleating drainpipe trousers fur lined parkas low waist dropped shoulders suede cardigans folds organic ripples wool blends cashmere hair effects bouclé poodle knits weaves sheer to double face qualities flannels stretch loden felted wools sand-wiched reverse coated delicate sheer textures mix nature man-made light fibrous sheer trans-parent lustre matt embroidery chain stitch romantic quality florals in colour scale digital images urban monotonal.

Case Study – Research Direction

detachable sleeves and strap

Yohji Yamamoto

lace wrap

simple cowl back

contemporary and archive designers

slate and stone fastenings

Yohji Yamamoto

three furs mixed

batwing

Comme des Garçons

transparent black pockets

fluidity and utility

contemporary designers

transparency and utility

asymmetry and utility

Vivienne Westwood

Summer 2000

Christian Lacroix

gingham and floral

black spots

broad belt

glitter buckle

irridescent fringe

Case Study – Research Direction

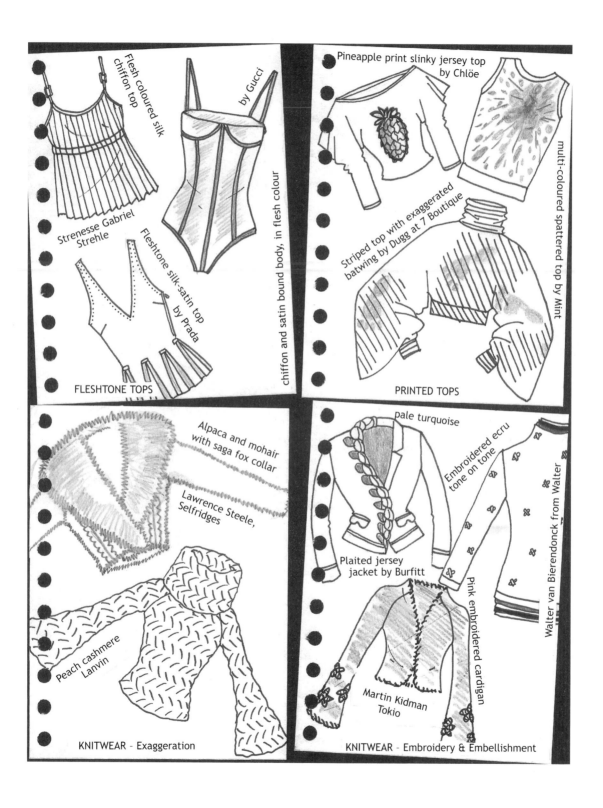

Flesh coloured silk chiffon top

by Gucci

Strenesse Gabriel Strehle

Fleshtone silk-satin top by Prada

chiffon and satin bound body, in flesh colour

FLESHTONE TOPS

Pineapple print slinky jersey top by Chlöe

multi-coloured spattered top by Mint

Striped top with exaggerated batwing by Dugg at 7 Boutique

PRINTED TOPS

Alpaca and mohair with saga fox collar

Lawrence Steele, Selfridges

Peach cashmere Lanvin

KNITWEAR – Exaggeration

pale turquoise

Embroidered ecru tone on tone

Walter van Bierendonck from Walter

Plaited jersey jacket by Burfitt

Pink embroidered cardigan

Martin Kidman Tokio

KNITWEAR – Embroidery & Embellishment

Case Study – Research Direction

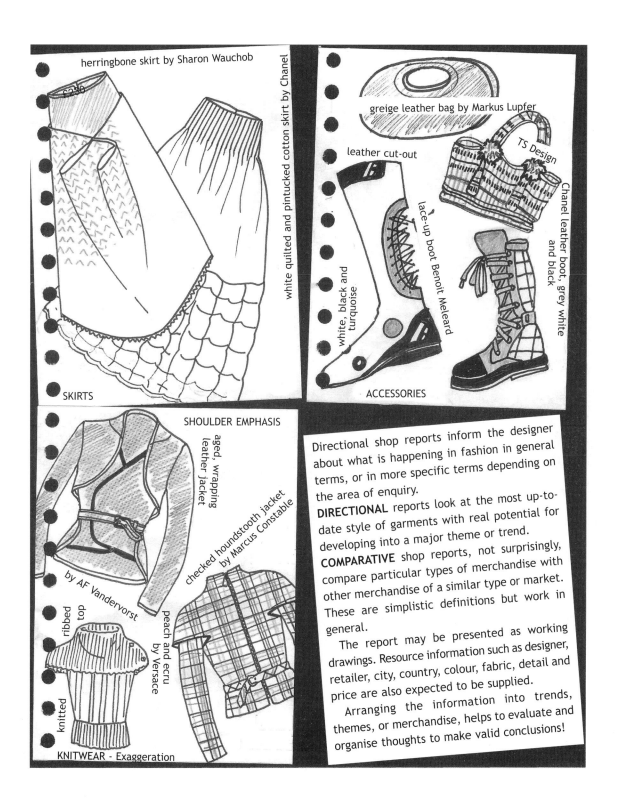

herringbone skirt by Sharon Wauchob

white quilted and pintucked cotton skirt by Chanel

SKIRTS

greige leather bag by Markus Lupfer

leather cut-out

white, black and turquoise

lace-up boot Benoit Meleard

TS Design

Chanel leather boot, grey white and black

ACCESSORIES

SHOULDER EMPHASIS

aged, wrapping leather jacket

checked houndstooth jacket by Marcus Constable

by AF Vandervorst

ribbed top

peach and ecru by Versace

knitted

KNITWEAR - Exaggeration

Directional shop reports inform the designer about what is happening in fashion in general terms, or in more specific terms depending on the area of enquiry.

DIRECTIONAL reports look at the most up-to-date style of garments with real potential for developing into a major theme or trend.

COMPARATIVE shop reports, not surprisingly, compare particular types of merchandise with other merchandise of a similar type or market. These are simplistic definitions but work in general.

The report may be presented as working drawings. Resource information such as designer, retailer, city, country, colour, fabric, detail and price are also expected to be supplied.

Arranging the information into trends, themes, or merchandise, helps to evaluate and organise thoughts to make valid conclusions!

Case Study – Fabric Development

chain stitch

cream on grey

Ben Hall's denim hooked rugs

washed-up arran

Eco Deco

naïve textiles and architectural influences

from In Touch by Kelly Hoppen

machine stitching

gold cut away cream on velvet

seeds on sticks

'the whale coming close to the shore'

Janet Bolton from 3 fishes 5 stars

contemporary Japanese Design by Sian Evans

Case Study – Fabric Development

A variety of fabric stories were developed for the case study. After the research some preliminary colour work was done and then the fabric stories were created. The stories were devised in colour. Each fabric story measured 19 cm by 15 cm; there were seven plates. Whilst a time-consuming task, this was also a very stimulating and helpful task as it allowed for a lot of preliminary decision making and editing.

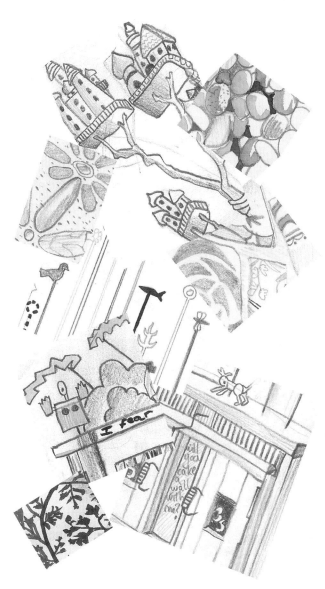

COLOUR:
Black, Turquoise, Ecru, Silver.

FUR AND FEATHERS MIXED, APPLIQUÉ, TEXTURAL MIXES:
Mother of pearl, lace appliqué over taffeta with glass beading and mirror tiles, ethnic beaded tassels, cotton jersey with beaded swirl embroidery, tufted fake fur, welded quilting, naïve figurative buttons.

The inspiration was revisited to devise a colour story. There were many possibilities. The colour stories were tested by being developed through into fabric. In fact, it does not make a lot of sense to develop colour without reference to available fabrics, unless a lot of dyeing is an objective.

Case Study – Fabric Development

A. COLOUR:
Charcoal, Navy, Ecru, White, Beige.

B. COLOUR:
Charcoal, Silver, Ecru, White, Greige.

C. COLOUR:
Navy, Ecru, Inky Blue, Mole, Gold.

A: NAÏVE PATTERNS AND RANDOM BEADING, SIMPLISTIC SHAPES:
Drawn thread and beading, simple seedling embroidery with matt beading, brushed jersey, voile with naïve appliqué, chunky knit with naïve beading, figured jacquard with hessian and lace appliqué.

B: INTRODUCTION OF TECHNOLOGICALLY INSPIRED TEXTILES, SHARP EDGES, GEOMETRY:
'Magic Touch'* architectural print on velvet, 'Magic Touch' architectural print on voile, fine knife pleats welded in PVC, PVC with shaped darts, random welding and shaped pleating, fine tucks in PVC.

C: NATURAL AND DRY HANDLE, SOFT, FLUFFY, FLAT:
Loosely knitted chenille yarn, dry handle, bound buttons, cotton velvet with beading and random embroidery, metallic swirl appliqué, bias binding – dry/matt handle, mother of pearl, embellished checks, silk velvet with chenille swirl embroidery.

* Magic Touch is a trade name for photocopy transfer paper.

Case Study – Fabric Development

A. COLOUR:
Gold, Charcoal, Silver, Mole, Ecru, Pea-Green.

B. COLOUR:
Pale Yellow, Turquoise, Ecru, Red, Pink, Lime, Gold, Black, Charcoal.

A: HARD SUBSTANCES, BEADING AND PVC, MESHES, CUT-OUTS:
Mirror tile and glass bead embroidery, white naïve print, lime-washed pigskin, foil embossing, lace PVC welded on to sparkle PVC, mosaic square-bead appliqué with gold thread, pigskin and glove suede.

B: NAÏVE EMBROIDERY AND PATCHWORK EFFECTS:
Transparent inserts, silk velvet with random embroidery, beaded tassles, ceramic buttons, mother of pearl, oilskin with beaded trims and braid, seedling embroidery on rayon taffeta, slubbed silk with naïve embroidery and beading.

C: ETHNIC INFLUENCES, MATT AND SPARKLE, CHECKS AND LINES:
Patchwork gingham/checks, fantasy buttons, tufted ribbed fleece, experimental pleating with beading, double-faced fleece, ripstop nylon coated with rubber, slubbed silk, glass mosaic decoration, multi-coloured buttons, cotton fringing, transparency with embroidery.

C. COLOUR:
Navy, Sky Blue, Ecru, Red, White, Pale Blue, Lime, Yellow, Lilac, Gold.

Case Study – Design Development

decorative buttons

funnel neck in jersey

extra long sleeves

gathers over bust

mesh & bead embroidery

back view

drawn thread with beads

extra long sleeves rouched up

double faced fleece

white or turquoise beading on ecru

cream check

cream on cream print

jacquard with hessian and lace applique

naturals ecru & beige

cream & black mosaic print

black fringe

welded quilting

quilted shoulders

ecru mohair & cotton knit

embroidered inset

sleeveless overdress/coat

embroidered waist

pigskin jacket

tinted fur

beaded stars

jersey

bellows pocket

Case Study – Design Development

beaded detail

long sleeved top

floral print - grand scale

elasticated banding

stretch top with gusset

chunky knit with cut-outs

fitted beaded top

decorative beading

back view

graphic print

halter neck

beaded gusset

back view

quilted, moulded top

beaded detail

ecru/naturals with dark accents

with cut-outs

double faced fleece top

concealed fasten

top with fringing

knitted dress

voile

mesh gusset

embroidered front

etched copper

swirly button brushed,

swirl embroidery

transparent sleevehead

Case Study – Design Development

naïve embroidery

back view

sleeveless top

back view

stretch top

fur trim - astrakhan

...s t r e t c h y...

wrap

fringing or embroidery

cream jersey

asymmetry

asymmetry

kimono style

asymmetrical skirt

tone on tone embroidery

black on stone jersey

Case Study – Design Development

PVC welded

skirt with scallop trim

decorative beaded buttons

rectangular skirt with points - drape at the side in dramatic print

back view

printed gusset

front view

velvet trousers

wrap view

PVC trousers

gusset & wrap skirt give layered effect

large scale print

light weight fabric

feminine scallop detail

welded PVC

cut-out detail

PVC welded bag

saddle bag – hands free

jumpsuit with PVC welded top & stretch trouser

belt and purse in PVC

back view only

PVC welded pleated skirt

spiral type print on one leg

velvet trousers

splash print

wrap skirt in PVC

PVC welded top with single strap

177

Case Study – Design Development

front

architectural print on velvet

front

back

front

transparent insets

shaped welding in PVC

string handle

back

random PVC welding in 'sparkle'

PVC welding & cut-outs

layered tunic with

tucks-PVC welding

rope handle

mesh spiral baskets

asymmetry

PVC welding with

PVC lace insets

credit cards,

mobile phones

loose change

detachable purses

random pleating & PVC welding in 'sparkle'

back view

patchwork skirt

welded tucks

velvet architectural print top

pleating with welds

foil patches

cut out sleeve faced with fabric

Case Study – Design Development

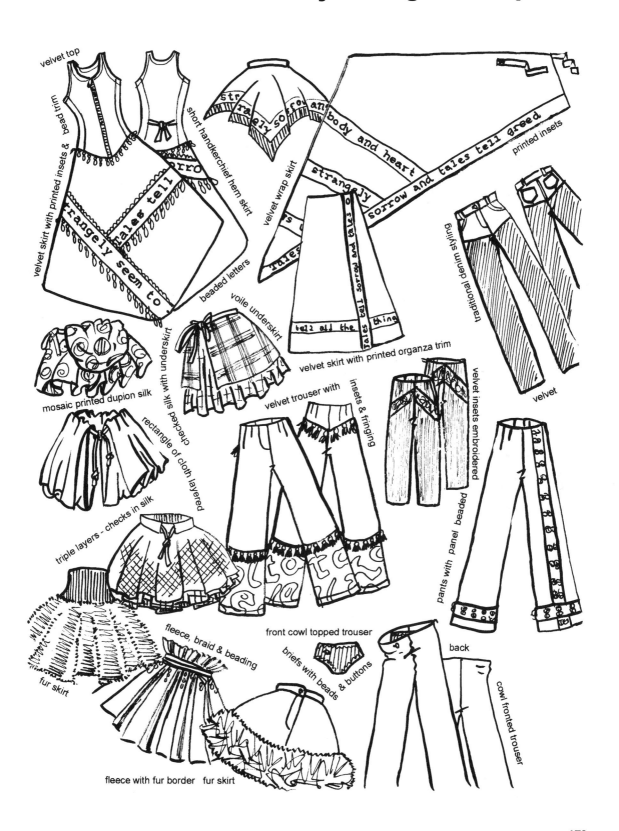

velvet top

short handkerchief hem skirt

bead trim

velvet skirt with printed insets & beaded letters

strangely sorrow anybody and heart

strangely sorrow and tales tell greed

printed insets

velvet wrap skirt

traditional denim styling

velvet

voile underskirt

velvet skirt with printed organza trim

mosaic printed dupion silk

checked silk with underskirt

rectangle of cloth layered

velvet trouser with insets & fringing

velvet insets embroidered

Pants with panel beaded

triple layers - checks in silk

front cowl topped trouser

fleece, braid & beading

briefs with beads & buttons

back

fur skirt

fleece with fur border   fur skirt

cowl fronted trouser

Case Study – Design Development

jeans detailing

jeans styling mixed with pattern

patchwork mosaic blue on cream

back view

spiral wrap skirt

layer over pants and skirt

spiral appliquéd patch with tufting

quilted rectangle

embroidered organza layered straps

spirals 'tales'

swirly beaded pattern

four rectangles skirt

knitted jacket with embroidery

tipped fur

sleeveless

traditional jean's styling

beaded stars

ecru denim

the updated twinset

zip front

beading and tassles

transparent visor

kagoule with dipped back

stretch ribbing undersleeve

tone on tone printed

fur hood & cuffs

zip off extra long sleeves

natural oilskin

velvet

asymmetric sash tie

decorative borders

contrasting fabric velvet & mohair

organic print

contrasting belt - printed

side zips

surface texture,

decorative beading

embroidered swirls

Case Study – Design Development

white on white embroidery

oilskin & fur

beaded kagoule

oilskin

organza ribbon-embroidered

tabard effect

printed belt-cummerbund

printed lining beaded border

hooded anorak with check borders

pocket flap

printed wrap fasten

quilted coat

beaded hem & front

ripstop nylon

pigskin coat in ecru

angular shoe in leather

fully beaded upper

full leather lace up

boot in 'sparkle'

welded PVC sunburst

backless boot with straps

beaded mohair scarf with tassles

printed silk scarf

embroidered sash belt with silk ties

CHANGE

shawl scarf with mosaic print in natural colours

'poodle' boot

embroidered saddle bags

cummerbund style beaded and embroidered

knitted balaclava with beads and zip

soft felt sombrero

with printed babushka

striped knitted stocking cap

trompe l'oeil bag derived from cupboard & matching purse

chunky sun glasses

fur Russian style hat with balaclava and metal earpieces

knitted ecru hat with beaded stars

soft leather bag with stone & slate fasten

chunky knitted duffle bag with slate and stone

printed leather bag

details & rope handles

The design development provides a 'snapshot' of what is expected in terms of quantity; for a collection a lot more work would be needed regarding initial ideas

183

Case Study – Design Development – Outfits

Layering of separates is a key direction for this collection; bold prints are used and placed in unusual positions (back of the trousers). A combination of soft, comfortable fabrics (wools, stretches and fleeces) and hard-edged fabrics (PVC) are used for contrast and to indicate the adverse reaction to cyberspace (soft fabrics) but also to remind us that technology exists (PVC). Text prints spiral up one trouser leg only.

Case Study – Design Development – Outfits

Cagoules for outerwear and fitted, zipped jackets for comfort – embellished with beading. Body wrapping with a printed shawl and bustle shape emphasise the torso. Oversized swirls add texture to customised denim. The text print wraps around a square-cut skirt, upside down. Trousers can be wide and printed or narrow and flared at the ankle. The overall look is long with interruptions by layering.

Case Study – Design Development – Outfits

Long A-line garments with asymmetrical hemlines, wrapping and draping effects. Mixed print and pattern with embroidered embellishment, floral, text and abstract swirls mixed together in a tone-on-tone colour palette. Fur trim, fringing and knits mixed in a utilitarian manner.

Case Study – Design Development – Outfits

Outerwear is full length but allows for glimpses of designs underneath. Different levels are achieved by developing simple shapes into complicated constructions; large prints complicate this effect. A simple print is interrupted by an unexpected splash of text. The PVC pinafore is lined with an oversized print to add interest when movement occurs. Mixes of fabrics, textures and patterns allow for a 'sensual' approach. Asymmetrical details (blouse sleeve) add an element of surprise.

Case Study – Outfits – Childrenswear

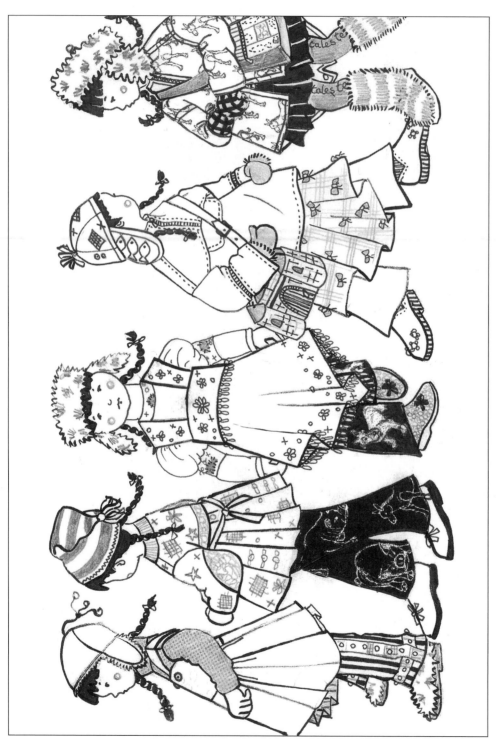

The same research material was used as inspiration for the development of a childrenswear collection, as much to save space in the book as anything, but although the fabric story could be interpreted easily for children, the print story was not necessarily entirely appropriate (see later in the Case Study).

Case Study – Outfits – Childrenswear

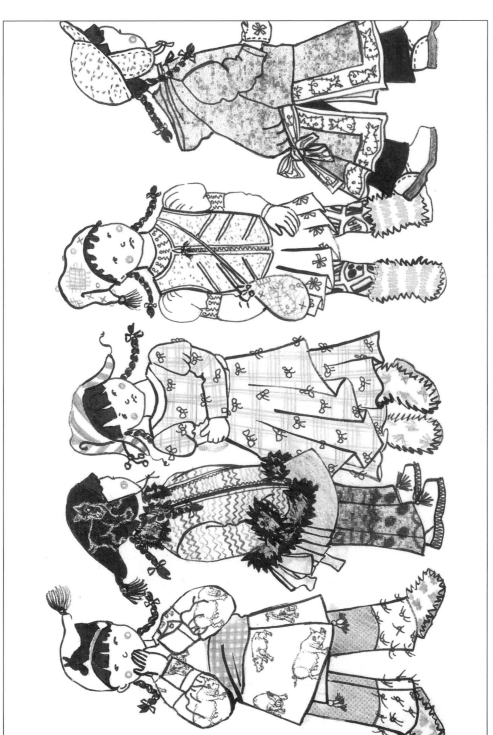

The same silhouettes were developed as for womenswear, with minor modifications, often with the main garments being shorter for practical reasons, allowing children to play without getting caught up in metres of fabric. The collection is essentially girlswear but could be adapted for boys also. The child would be about 2 to 4½ years old. By this time children do start to have an opinion about what they will wear and individual pieces could be bought rather than adopting the total look. The longer shapes could be used for partywear and special events when more items may be bought.

Case Study – Outfits – Childrenswear

What kind of print would be appropriate? It would have been possible to develop the floral theme, but somehow it seemed too sophisticated for children. The ideal solution seemed to be using animals. Children seem to love identifying animals and they offer an opportunity to introduce a more 'sketchy', textural approach to the prints.

The focus is interesting construction but without the oversized prints as these could overwhelm a child's proportions. Lots of small details are included to make each item desirable, whether it be by using gussets, asymmetry, fabric contrasts or beading and appliqué.

Case Study – Outfits – Childrenswear

The babies range from birth to 2 years old.

Shapes had to be seriously curtailed for babieswear. They need to be able to crawl and stand without stepping on their clothing. Traditional shapes like all-in-ones, dungarees and leggings work because they are comfortable and functional. Torso-length separates, with pretty trims and print/pattern contrast, work best. There are less applied trims here for safety reasons. The animal print works in a variety of scales – as overall prints, placed prints and border prints.

The animal print can also be contrived into fun shapes in garment construction and allow the child to become interested in what they are wearing (donkey and pig dungarees).

Case Study – Print Development – Childrenswear

Initial animal drawings were made from stylised animal toys. Different views of the animals were sketched to get an overall understanding of their anatomy. These drawings are then put into repeat to see how they will work as prints.

Case Study – Print Development – Childrenswear

Different techniques are tried, such as monoprint for a textural effect and 'greying' the outline to make it look softer. Spots are added to the animals to give them personality!

Case Study – Print Development – Childrenswear

PRINT DEVELOPMENT FOR CHILDRENSWEAR DESIGN

Print development requires thought regarding repeat patterns, colour, scale and proportion for successful final use of the textiles. Printed textiles can be very sophisticated nowadays, with photo-realistic images or the antithesis, hand-rendered, naive finishes.

The original drawing is rendered in black ink. The drawing is taken from a model of a terrier.

To save time in creating repeats, and using different media, the image is scanned into a computer and a variety of filters (in Adobe PhotoShop) are applied. The background shows a monoprint to achieve a rough/rustic effect, in keeping with the fabric stories developed earlier. The image is reduced and repeated and 'swirls' from the original inspiration are applied to the dog.

It is important to keep referring back to the research material for continuity in the collection.

Experimentation with colour is important in print development and here direction would be taken from the fabric stories. The textiles could be beaded and embroidered when completed, depending on the age of the child.

Case Study – Print Development – Childrenswear

Drawing and painting techniques can be used to great effect when developing printed textiles. Prints can be 'all-over', 'placed' or 'border prints'. Printed textiles can be further embellished with other surface decoration techniques.

The original dog is repeated and reversed to allow for a normal print repeat (this is 'one-way' only and could be an expensive print due to the limitations of cutting fabric that has one direction only!).

A filter is applied in Adobe PhotoShop – Artistic-Dry Brush – giving a rough but clearer finish.

The image is further experimented with by inverting it to white on a black background.

The experiments shown would be kept in a sketchbook for reference and would be referred to when designing to achieve a 'balance' of scale and effects.

Case Study – Print Development – Childrenswear

A variety of approaches are shown; the print is inverted, showing the silhouette of the animal only. The print has an embossing filter added in Adobe PhotoShop, to give a three-dimensional feeling. The line drawing is inverted and scratchy stars are added – derived from the fabric stories. The line drawing has beaded stars added. The animals are coloured and stripes are added to the background. The scale of the print is reduced. The animals have spots and stripes added for a bit of fun.

These are just initial ideas for print development. Print design requires a whole input of its own if designers want a lot of original print work in their collections. They would probably have to work with a textile designer, or buy textile designs from a trade fair or other selling event.

highlights are added as a watercolour wash

Case Study – Working Drawing

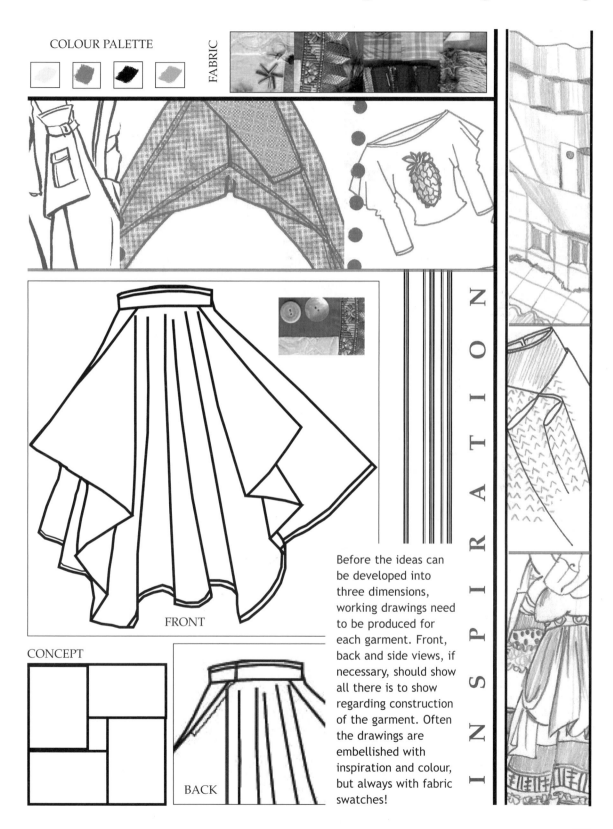

COLOUR PALETTE

FABRIC

FRONT

CONCEPT

BACK

INSPIRATION

Before the ideas can be developed into three dimensions, working drawings need to be produced for each garment. Front, back and side views, if necessary, should show all there is to show regarding construction of the garment. Often the drawings are embellished with inspiration and colour, but always with fabric swatches!

Case Study – Prototyping

PROTOTYPING - CREATING THE TOILE

Up till now, experimentation has been on paper. It is time to try the garments in three dimensions. For the purpose of this exercise a skirt will be investigated. The intial pattern is created and the pattern pieces are cut out of calico to make a 'toile'.

The skirt chosen is of a very simple construction. It is a series of four large rectangles stitched together as the working drawing.

Problems encountered: A very simple concept does pose some difficult problems; for example, the rectangles are easily stitched together but the points meeting the waist band are very acute and adding the waistband is problematic. It is necessary to try a sample to resolve this issue. Similarly, the fastening – a zip – should be easy to place, but the seams hang either side of the centre front. Rather than setting a zip into the cloth where there is no natural opening, it would be better to set it in one of the seams. It was decided to use the back left seam. This would also allow the waistband to sit flatteringly on the waist without any 'lumpiness' at the side.

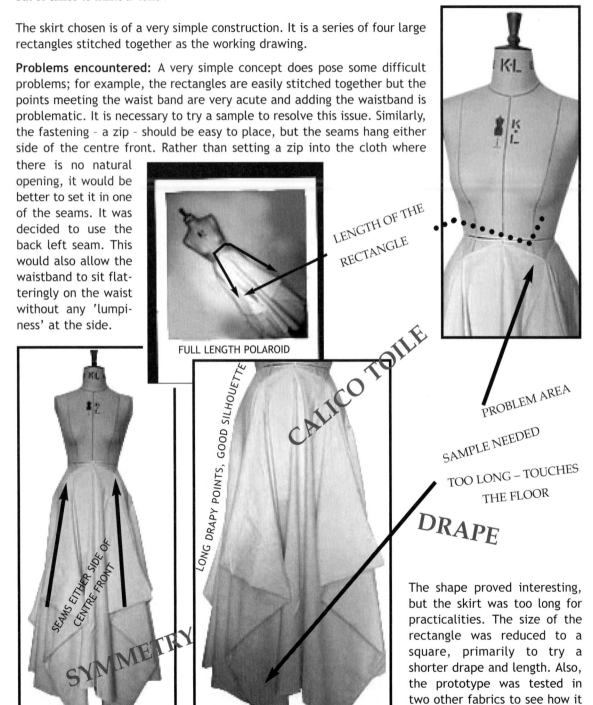

FULL LENGTH POLAROID

LENGTH OF THE RECTANGLE

CALICO TOILE

PROBLEM AREA

SAMPLE NEEDED

TOO LONG – TOUCHES THE FLOOR

DRAPE

LONG DRAPY POINTS, GOOD SILHOUETTE

SEAMS EITHER SIDE OF CENTRE FRONT

SYMMETRY

The shape proved interesting, but the skirt was too long for practicalities. The size of the rectangle was reduced to a square, primarily to try a shorter drape and length. Also, the prototype was tested in two other fabrics to see how it would behave.

Case Study – Prototyping

The shape of the garment proved interesting in its draping qualities and the silhouette subsequently created. The prototype was developed into two different fabrics: a nylon ciré for its clinging and fluid qualities and the complete antithesis, a padded, waterproofed outerwear fabric.

The sample was created using the padded outerwear fabric. It was bulky to work with and perceived as the most challenging of the fabrics; however, the results were achieved quite easily.

Note the difference in silhouette. The pattern was modified to produce a square rather than a rectangle and this consequently shortened the skirt.

The silhouette became more extreme when using both fabrics.

No other samples were required. It would be anticipated that a variety of finishes would be attempted if the fabric was new to the user!

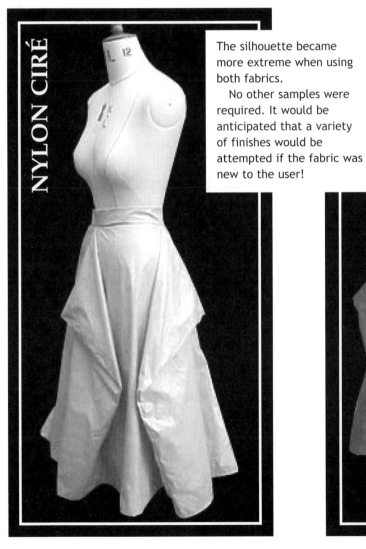

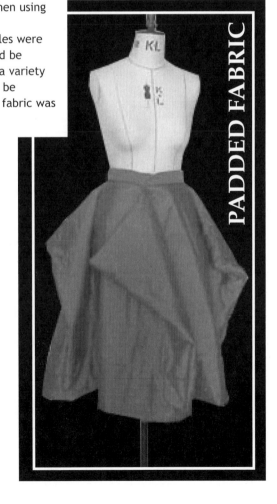

Case Study – Promotion/Graphics

The first step for promoting a range or collection is to choose a name that epitomises the philosophy. The name was chosen here by extracting key words from the personal philosophy and then using a thesaurus and dictionary to find words that were more poetic, pure or plain and simple.

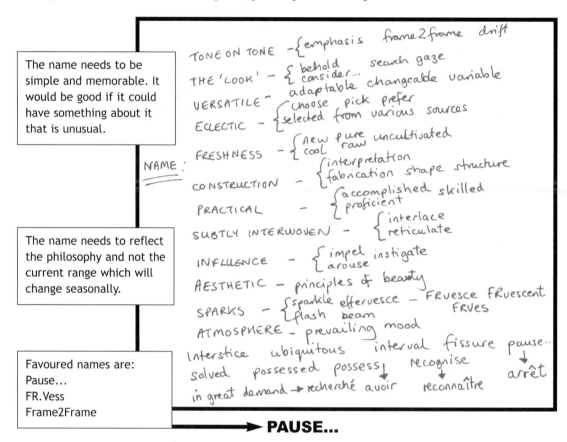

The name needs to be simple and memorable. It would be good if it could have something about it that is unusual.

The name needs to reflect the philosophy and not the current range which will change seasonally.

Favoured names are:
Pause...
FR.Vess
Frame2Frame

➤ **PAUSE...**

Why choose Pause...? It is simple; it asks the consumer to stop for a moment; it will allow for changes of direction in the future, for example Pause2 (Diffusion) or Pause for Men.... FR.Vess is too contrived, Frame2Frame does not suggest a fashion range. The word is then 'dressed up' in a 'font' or 'typeface' to achieve an identity. The following are basic fonts; free fonts can be found on the Internet and installed on your own computer.

Pause... *Pause*... Pause...**Pause**... Pause... **Pause...**
PAUSE...**Pause**...**Pause**...Pause...Pause...Pause... *Pause...*
Pause...Pause...Pause... Pause... Pause... Pause...
Pause...Pause...Pause ... Pause... *Pause* ... Pause ... Pause...
Pause ... Pause...Pause ... *Pause*...**Pause...**Pause ... Pause...
Pause...Pause...Pause...Pause...Pause...Pause...Pause... *Pause*

Case Study – Promotion/Graphics

Pause...
Sand 16pt

Pause...
New Berolina MT 16pt

Pause...
Trebuchet MS 16pt

The chosen font gives a relaxed and 'hand-written' effect. It works well in different scales. The task now is to apply it, to develop the hypothetical 'corporate identity' of the company and then apply that identity to the different scenarios where it may be used. The following pages show rough design ideas followed by a selection process and design development on the computer.

Sand 48pt

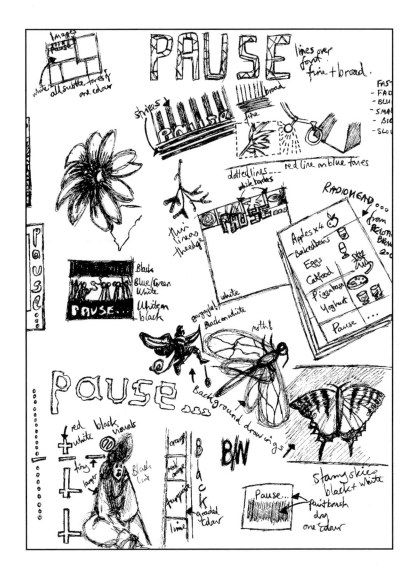

Case Study – Promotion/Graphics

Design ideas sheets need to be lively and enjoyable to produce. When looking at research material it is often more stimulating to draw the ideas than produce a sketchbook full of scraps. However, scraps may be useful for reference regarding colour and sophisticated finishes.

Case Study – Promotion/Graphics

Resources used for research are: magazines (fashion, graphics and technology); advertisements, both moving (television) and still; garment swing tickets; CD-ROM packaging including music; packaging; in fact anything with contemporary graphics. Surprisingly, graphics from 10 years ago were also reviewed to add another dimension to the work, combining old and new to give a fresher approach.

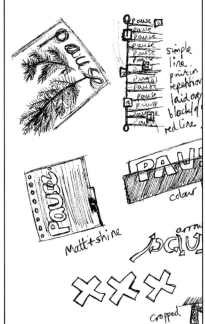

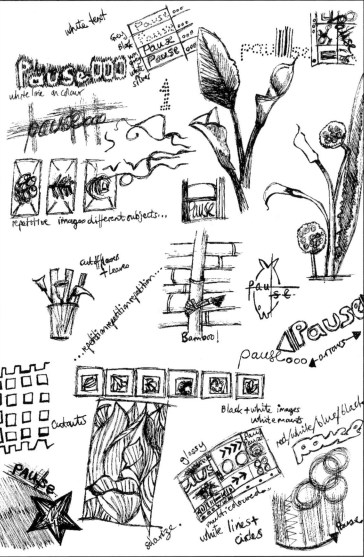

This research is essential before real development work can begin and is similar to the initial sketches required before garment development commences. Observation and recording cannot be over-emphasised!

Case Study – Promotion/Graphics

SELECTING IDEAS FOR FURTHER DEVELOPMENT

From the design ideas sheets, the most favoured ideas are selected for rendering on the computer. Editing the design development sheets with the end customer or client very much in mind, helps to focus on ideas that could work well. The idea needs to communicate strongly the identity that is desired, with no ambiguities, unless that is part of the design brief.

See the colour section on pages 207–18 to see how the promotion can be developed in colour.

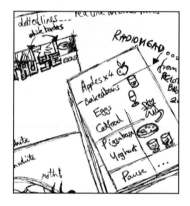

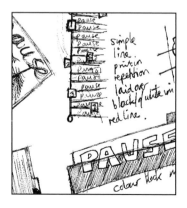
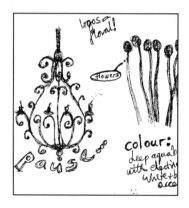

Case Study – Promotion/Graphics

Development begins on the computer. Adobe Photoshop software is used to edit and manipulate images taken with a digital camera. QuarkXpress software (for desktop publishing) is then used to display and develop designs by pulling visuals and text together to achieve the right kind of balance. Colour work is essential here.

A circular shape seemed to provide a useful starting point; lines and stripes were also introduced, derived from the ideas sheets. Drawings were layered and shadowed; this gives a more complex approach to the design.

Case Study – Promotion/Graphics

Images of plants and flowers are important influences to the case study. They fit into the 'planet earth meets technology' philosophy of the collection by mixing clean photography with a hand-rendered textured effect in the font.

Case Study – Promotion/Graphics

A variety of ever more layered designs. Do they communicate clearly? Do they look good?

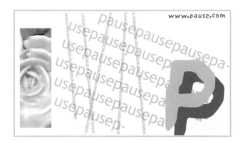

Case Study – Promotion/Graphics

The use of hand-rendered work and clean photography is mixed by using the drawings from the ideas sheets. The drawings are inverted for a softer feeling and the word 'Pause' is manipulated to make it less formal looking.

Photographic images are inverted to give an ethereal, almost unreal feeling. Font colours and backgrounds are inspired by the photography.

Case Study – Promotion/Graphics

Pages 211–214 show some of the final corporate identity ideas for the label.

Stationery – Letterhead

P A U S E...

Pause Headquarters
Eclectic House
Inspiration Avenue
Wonderland
WC10 NS99

Mr. Big Buyer,
Huge Department
Store,
Biggest Street
Capital City

Dear Sir,
Thankyou for your letter dated 23/5/2001. We very much appreciate your opinion and are pleased that you are delighted with your most recent order. We would be happy to repeat the order and offer our best service always.

Yours sincerely

Kathryn McKelvey

Creative Director
Pause...

www.pause.com
T. 0191 227 0000 F. 0191 227 0001 E. pause@pause.com

Business card

Kathryn McKelvey
Creative Director
T. 0191 227 0000 F. 0191 227 0001 E. pause@pause

Hanger label

Pause
Medium

Pocket-sized postcard

Case Study – Promotion/Graphics

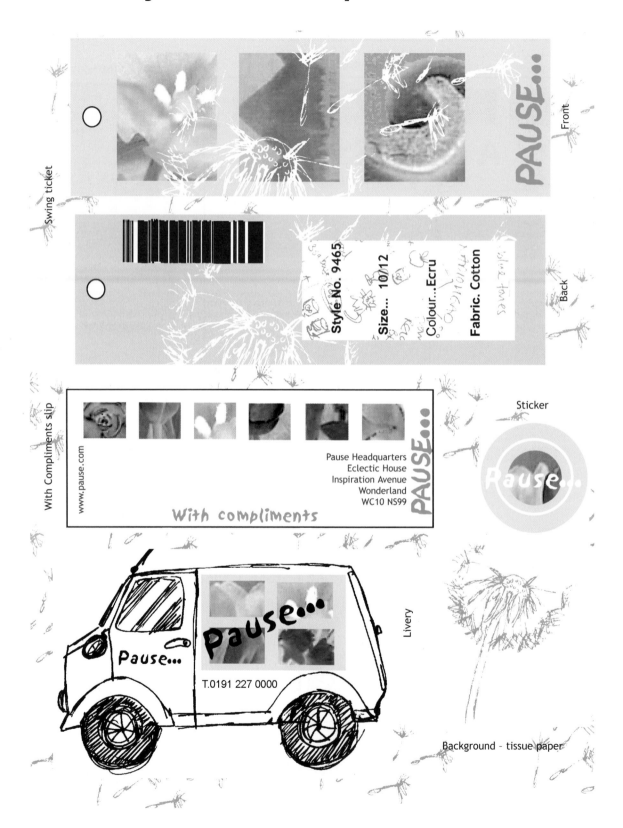

Swing ticket

Front

Back

Style No. 9465

Size... 10/12

Colour...Ecru

Fabric. Cotton

PAUSE...

With Compliments slip

www.pause.com

Pause Headquarters
Eclectic House
Inspiration Avenue
Wonderland
WC10 NS99

PAUSE...

With compliments

Sticker

Pause...

Livery

Pause...

Pause...

T.0191 227 0000

Background – tissue paper

Case Study – Promotion/Graphics

The previous two pages show the final 'corporate identity' for the label. The final products include stationery ideas with letterhead, business card, with compliments slip and delivery vehicle livery. The promotional material consists of a postcard, swing ticket, hanger label, tissue paper for wrapping and a sticker. This page shows packaging development ideas and the final product, including long carriers with shoulder straps for larger items, a box for packing accessories and a smaller bag for smaller items. While in this book we can only consider shapes and visuals, it is also important to look at the materials and construction of the designs. Should they have a matt or shiny finish, a textural or smooth finish?

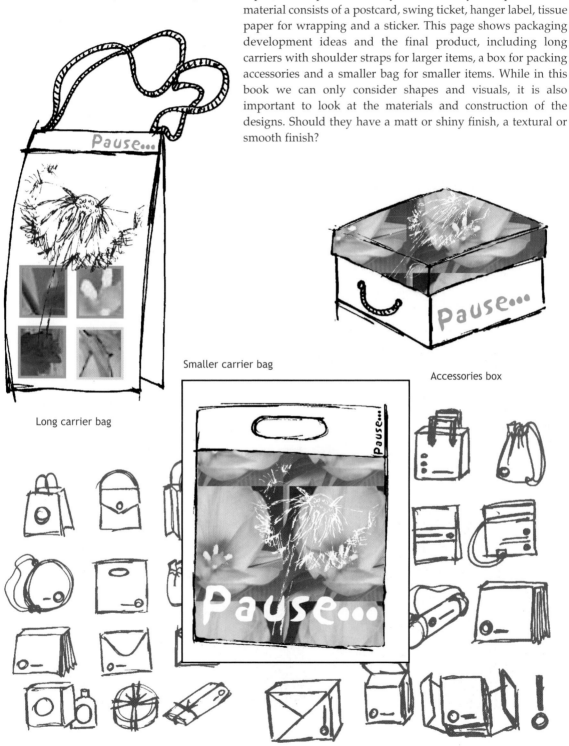

Long carrier bag

Smaller carrier bag

Accessories box

Case Study – Promotion/Graphics

How many colours should be used? What should the handles be made from? The answers here depend upon the market level and the budget. Think about laminating, PVC or acetate covers, frosted vinyls, tracing paper overlays, embossed finishes, embossed foils, hand-made papers, layers, corrugated papers and cards, metallic card, perspex, welded PVC, transparency with overprints, string, yarn, cords ...

This page shows more packaging, this time for mail order and a mail order catalogue. The identity is applied to both designs for continuity. The mail-order brochure is square and folds as a 'concertina'. Each page works as a double-page spread and then repeats the format in a variety of ways. The styling photographs are included here. The photographs need to be clear for ordering. The packaging below is for small items that need packing as gifts or for hygiene purposes.

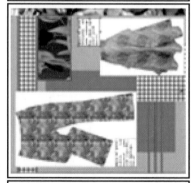

Gift packaging

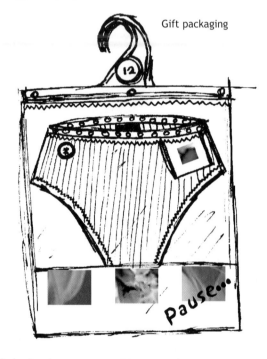

Mail Order Brochure - cover and two spreads

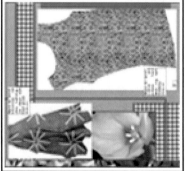

Case Study – Promotion/Graphics

Part of the graphic designer's job may be selling from the page – nowadays a very popular way of selling merchandise in a competitive market place. As the design disciplines blur it is a good opportunity to investigate your talents in selling your own designs.

All of the garments here are hypothetical, created with new technology! From the prototype skirts and some improvised clothing shapes the following pages were 'mocked-up'. Some of the original floral images that were used in the graphics were used here also for continuity, as well as to reinforce the 'identity' that has been created.

Style No. A0001
Unusually cut ciré rectangular skirt with bead print.
£120-00

Style No. A0001
Cotton and mohair hand knit top with beading.
£200-00

3

Case Study – Promotion/Graphics

The background of the page was created in Adobe Illustrator and was then imported into QuarkXpress. The garments were created in Adobe PhotoShop. By photographing the prototype skirts and some other basic items of clothing with a digital camera, the photographic images could then be worked over with the 'polygon tool' and the 'pattern stamp tool', after scanning a variety of fabric textures, prints and patterns from the original fabric stories in the case study.

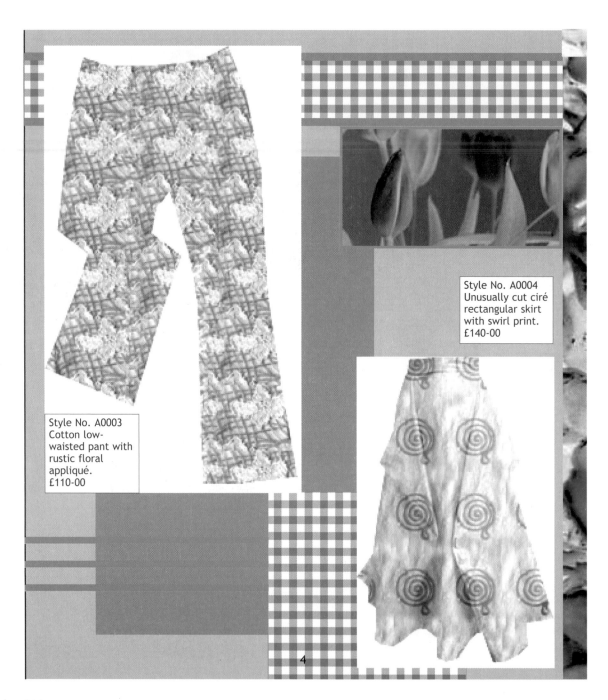

Style No. A0004
Unusually cut ciré
rectangular skirt
with swirl print.
£140-00

Style No. A0003
Cotton low-
waisted pant with
rustic floral
appliqué.
£110-00

4

216

Case Study – Promotion/Graphics

Extra details were applied to the page layout using QuarkXpress, including the page numbers, stripes of colour, photographic images, text, borders and the garment images themselves.

The layout is supposed to evoke very 'clean' graphics that are relevant for the market intended.

Style No. A0005
Embroidered, silk
velvet, padded
rectangular skirt.
£220-00

Style No. A0006
Printed cotton
jersey T-shirt
with contrast
printed bands.
£80-00

5

Case Study – Promotion/Graphics

Creating a piece of work like this requires a great deal of improvisation. How do you communicate 'fashion' without using models, who undoubtedly can sell garments very successfully?

The prototype skirts were photographed on a dress stand. The treatment with the computer software does stiffen the whole effect a little, but the overall look was what was required. Also, as this is a prototype catalogue, more detailed design decision making could be done at a later date.

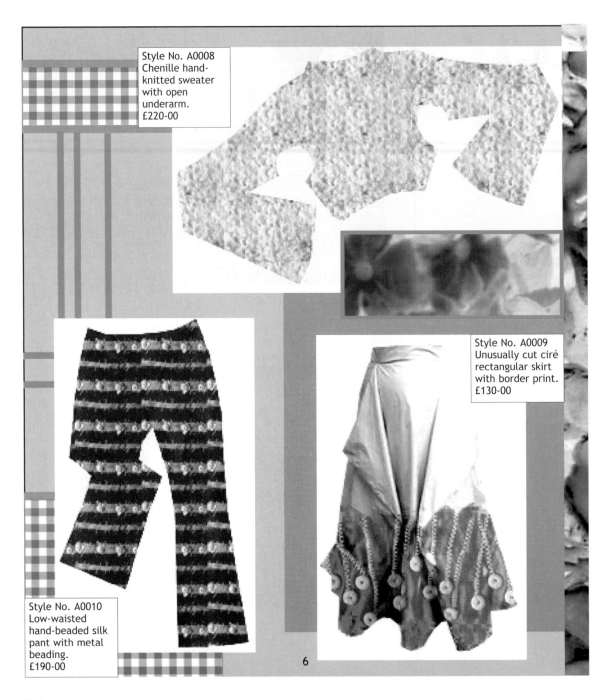

Style No. A0008
Chenille hand-knitted sweater with open underarm.
£220-00

Style No. A0009
Unusually cut ciré rectangular skirt with border print.
£130-00

Style No. A0010
Low-waisted hand-beaded silk pant with metal beading.
£190-00

6

Case Study – Promotion/Styling

Photographing a range is central to promoting it. Garments can show movement, proportion, length, drape and the effect of colour. The process for photographic styling is the same as that for any other design process: research, development, innovation/inspiration, final product. The final product will include graphic techniques.

Perspective and scale-architecture

Strong lighting or overexposed

Posed then overlayed with items

Half illustration, half photograph

Photo with illustration overlayed

Large illustration with photo collage

Case Study – Promotion/Styling

Magazines and advertising are used as research material to keep the styling looking contemporary. Different techniques are recorded. The most relevant will be used at the photographic shoot. Once the shoot is to be set up, a large quantity of tear sheets will be needed to provide information on backdrops and locations, and to plan poses, attitudes, lighting and make-up effects!

Photograph with 'wind or blur' filter

Mirror images, multiple images

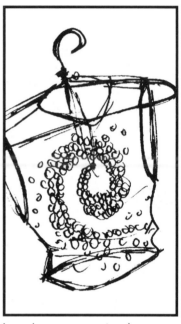

Large images, garment on hanger

Garments superimposed, not worn

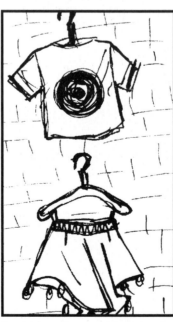

Garments on hanger against rusticity

Translucent layers

Case Study – Promotion/Styling

A combination of photographic imagery and illustration creates one of a series of promotional posters for the company.

Case Study – Promotion/Styling

The effect of the clean lines and blocks contrasts with the textural illustrations superimposed over the figure. The final **styling ideas** that were used were: half illustration, half photograph; translucent layers, posed then overlaid with items.

Case Study – Promotion/Styling

The posters would be used for promotional purposes in magazines and on billboards. The previous two poses were quite simple; this one is a little more active.

The poses are derived from sketches executed in the research inspiration stage and rendered as line drawings in Adobe Illustrator.

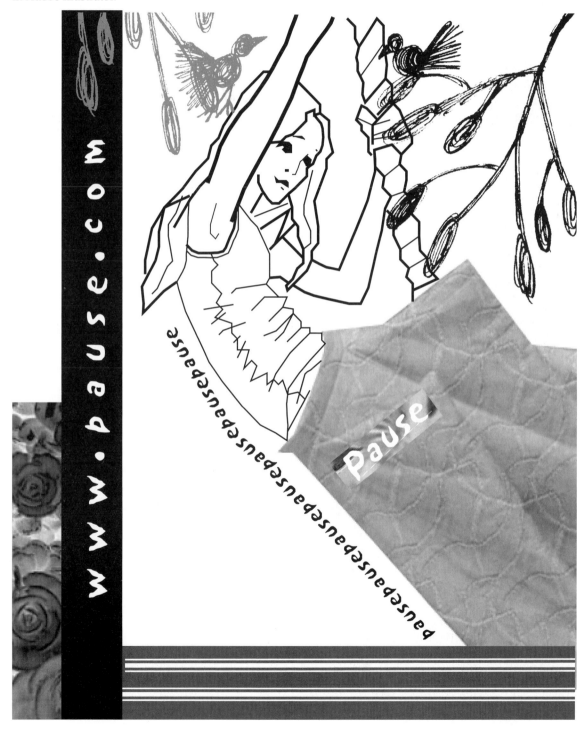

Bibliography

Some of these books and services have been used to support content; others are simply inspirational!

Adair, J. (1996) *Effective Innovation: How to Stay Ahead of the Competition*. Pan, London.

Baldizzone, T. & Baldizzone, G. (1995) *Tibet - on the Path of the Gentleman Brigands - Retracing the Steps of Alexandra David-Neel*. Thames & Hudson, London.

Borrelli, L. & Steele, V. (1999) *Bags - A Lexicon of Style*. Scriptum Editions, London.

Collings, M. (2000) *This is Modern Art*. Seven Dials, Cassell and Co., London.

Cox, C. (2000) *Lingerie - A Lexicon of Style*. Scriptum Editions, London.

Evans, S. (1991) *Contemporary Japanese Design*. Collins & Brown, London.

Fassett, K.& Bahouth, C. (1999) *Mosaics*. Ebury Press, London.

Goodman, M. (1995) *Creative Management*. Prentice Hall, London.

Gould, K. (2000) *Dishy*. Hodder & Stoughton, London.

Henry, J. (ed.) (1991) *Creative Management*. Sage, London (Sage is in Association with Open University).

Kelly, K. (1994) *Out of Control: The New Biology of Machines*. Fourth Estate, London.

McDowell, C. (1997) *Galliano*. Weidenfeld and Nicolson, London.

McKelvey, K. (1996) *Fashion Source Book*. Blackwell Publishing, Oxford.

McKelvey, K. & Munslow, J. (1997) *Illustrating Fashion*. Blackwell Publishing, Oxford.

Mauriès, P. (1996) *Christian Lacroix: The Diary of a Collection*. Thames & Hudson, London.

Newcastle Arts Centre Exhibition on Folk Tales, October–December 2000.

Norman, D.A. (1988) *The Psychology of Everyday Things*. Basic Books, USA.

Pavitt, J. (2000) *brand.new*. V & A Publications, London.

Petty, G. (1997) *How to be better at ... Creativity*. Kogan Page, London.

Popcorn, F. (1996) *Clicking*. Thorsons, London.

Popcorn, F. (1991) *The Popcorn Report*. Arrow Books, London.

Reiwoldt, O. (2000) *Retail Design*. Laurence King Publishing, London.

Roberts, R.M. (1989) *Serendipity, Accidental Discoveries in Science*. John Wiley & Sons Inc., USA.

Siler, T. (1997) *Think Like A Genius*. Bantam Press, London.

Sternberg, R.J. & Davidson, J.E. (eds) (1996) *The Nature of Insight*. MIT Press, MIT.

Stevens, M. (1996) *How to be a Better ... Problem Solver*. Kogan Page, London.

Symes, B. (1995) *Eureka! The Book of Inventing*. Headline Book Publishing, London.

Tenner, E. (1996) *Why Things Bite Back: The New Technology and the Revenge Effect*. Fourth Estate.

Textile View published quarterly by Metropolitan Publishing.

Tibor & Kalman, M. (2000) *(Un)Fashion*. Booth-Clibborn Editions, London.

Tilke, M. (1990) *Costume Patterns and Design*. Magna Books, Wigston, Leicester.

Van Grundy, A.B. (1988) *Techniques of Structured Problem Solving*. Van Nostrand Reinhold, New York.

Walton, S. & Walton, S. (2000) *Eco Deco*. Aquamarine, London.

Wells, W.D. & Prensky, D. (1996) *Consumer Behaviour*. John Wiley & Sons Inc., USA.

WGSN-edu.com   a trend resource from Worth Global Style Network based in London.

Widdows, L. & McGuinness, J. (1996) *Catwalk: Working with Models*. Batsford, London.

Index

Index